Stories and Poems from Solstice Shorts Festival 2017

Edited by Cherry Potts

ARACHNE PRESS

First published in UK 2018 by Arachne Press Limited
100 Grierson Road, London SE23 1NX
www.arachnepress.com
© Arachne Press 2018
ISBN:
Print: 978-1-909208-54-4
ePub: 978-1-909208-55-1
Mobi: 978-1-909208-57-5

Printed on wood-free paper in the UK by TJ International, Padstow.

Thanks to my fellow organisers:
Sherry, Mandy, Haworth, Colin, Barbara, Holly, Kirsty, Helen,
Anna, Katy, Thomas and Carl, and especially Yvonne, Phil and
Ness who also took on longlisting duties.
Thanks also to our funders:
Arts Council England, Feast, Cornwall Council, Nottingham
City Council, and all our crowdfund friends.

DUSK

Contents

Introduction

The Solstice Shorts Festival started in Greenwich on the prime meridian, on the shortest day of 2014, with an all-day Time-themed music and words extravaganza from sunrise to sunset. It reached its fourth year in 2017 and the time theme turned to *Dusk*. This is not a particularly audience friendly time of day, even when limited to the latest portion, *Astronomical* Dusk – that time when it is dark, but not dark enough to see the stars.

You can't have a 42 minute festival (can you?), so I decided to branch out and test an idea I've had since the inception of the festival – multiple sites.

Many tweets and emails and phone conversations (and false starts), followed. The idea evolved into BSL interpreted events at twelve sites, from pubs to arts centres and libraries, by way of woodlands and hillsides, and became the 2017 Solstice Shorts Festival: *Dusk – a wave of words across the UK.*

Starting with music in Ellon in Aberdeenshire at the moment of Solstice at 16:28 on 21st December 2017 and kicking off the stories and poems at 17:07, the festival raced over the country at the speed of dark, with overlapping events taking place (many with songs as well) in Inverness, Carlisle, Holyhead, Lancaster, Rossendale, Nottingham, Birmingham, Greenwich, Kelston, and Warkleigh, ending in Redruth in Cornwall as full dark fell at 18:20.

With a live video upload to Facebook throughout, the festival lasted barely one and a quarter hours, but produced almost nine hours of video. (I love this time stuff, it's so fluid.)

Dusk lends itself to the anxiety that darkness brings, so there is a fair smattering of edge-of-horror, chills-down-the-spine and keeping-the-lights-on, but there is also humour and the in-between-ness of the cusp of day when *anything* is possible.

STORIES

MacFarquhar's Bed
Alex Reece Abbott

The spring nor'wester blows steady and chill in MacFarquhar's face, but the early evening air is honeyed with golden gorse.

He strolls past the kirk and the sweet chestnuts that edge the town, hiking up the winding road. Every so often he turns, catching his breath and taking in the Cairngorms, still wearing their snowy caps. Cutting through the back of the raggle-taggle farm, he passes the little row of workers' cottages, and the old stone barn, where the cows low and moan.

He crosses the lush sloping fields, greeted by the tight-fleeced sheep and on the summit, he pauses in the soft gloaming and pulls out his brass eyeglass. The millpond Cromarty lies to his right and the Moray Firth to his left, but tonight the Moray is the sea inlet that holds his eye. On he ambles, down the avenue where the bark of the beech trees trails silvery, lichen beards. Their dark, wind-sculpted branches reach out for the sky, wild as the hair of Macbeth's crones.

When the town is an hour behind him, he creeps along the winding cliff, brushing by spiny gorse and boulders turned cushions by thick emerald moss. On, he traces a path that's narrow as a goat track and slippery as soap from the day's mizzling showers. Below him, waves drum in the new tide's arrival, smashing on the crumbling cornelian cliffs, drowning out the skylarks that serenade day's end. A red kite dances above him, watching his progress, hoping for a fall and fresh prey.

Finally, MacFarquhar reaches the stony beach, edging past the shell middens left by the old hunter-gatherers. He climbs the ancient nobbled sea arch that has formed in the rust-red sandstone, until he is above the glinting firth that's blue as the slate roof of his creel.

A pair of unblinking shags observe him, then carry on fishing; they are used to him by now. The turning tide exposes the fossil-rich outcrops, rocky fingers where fortune-seeking optimists come chancing their luck, hammering and chiselling through millennia.

Beneath him, the ocean has carved a well, an old chapel still adorned with scraps of cloth from townspeople seeking cures for their ailments and wanting to cast out evil spirits. The fulmars mock, their cackling amplified by the cliffs. MacFarquhar agrees; he is long past such foolish superstition.

Now he lies on the grassy outcrop bed, waiting for the dimming of the day. Some hate it drawing in, he loves it for obliterating.

From his lookout atop the arch, he scans the firth for a sign that his contraband is sailing his way, but all he spots is a pod of bottlenose dolphins. A gliding peregrine hunts for pigeons in the caves. As the wind picks up, he draws his length of plaid closer around his shoulders and closes his eyes for a moment.

Not all bad, he's self-made, a pirate, a smuggler. A man who has placed his faith in faster, easier, more certain ways to improve his fortune than wishes or fossils or prayers.

Night will fall. He embraces that certainty.

Breadcrumbs
Lucy Grace
Dusk, that time between day and night when everything changes...

The unexpected glittering took her breath, stilled her with tiny ice swords.

'Wow,' said Elizabeth. 'It's beautiful.'

'What?' asked John.

'The garden, look, it's all white.'

During the night a thick hoar frost had lain down to sleep outside. Creeping in the darkness, it had flowed silently over every external surface whilst they were closeted inside, a pale, immobilising lava.

'So you've not seen damn frost before, is that it? Always a fucking drama...' John yanked open the cutlery drawer with a metal rattle of tray bones. At the window Elizabeth folded her arms. She noted the single mug at the boiling kettle, the reflected solitary spoon tap-tap-tapping against the worktop.

'But it's pretty, though, don't you think?' She didn't know where this pleading came from.

Her grip on the sink edge tightened as thick sausage fingers circled her wrist. She cried out when the scalding metal teaspoon pressed as a reminder onto her arm, a burning watch face on a bracelet of bruises.

'What's for dinner tonight?' asked John.

Crossing to the fridge, Elizabeth knelt, her eye and cheek hidden by a curtain of hair, dulled and raggedly cut.

'We only have...' but on hearing the rude click of the key in the back door Elizabeth breathed again in the relief of an empty kitchen. Through the glass lay a thread of footprints, a million tiny ice crystals crushed and melted.

By 9.20 next morning the dirty green and urban greys had returned, the dawning wonderland disappeared. The chill window pressed Elizabeth's forehead into a smoothed plane. She shook free of emotion as the medication began to work, rolling over her limbs like hot bath water.

By 11.43 her tea was cold in the mug, a thin surface film adhering to the edges in a coarsening scum.

By 14.14 the day's brief winter sun had been and gone. Too weak to warm the earth or the sagging washing on the line, it had retreated, given up for another day.

By 16.55 the path to the pavement sparkled once more with sharp miniature gems, crunchy underfoot. Elizabeth sat on the freezing bricks of the low wall. Starlings chattered at her from the high wires as they gathered for a noisy bedtime outside the closed eyes of the houses opposite, doorway mouths double locked and bolted against callers. Her foot hurt – the broken glass had cut a red spider web on the sole. She ate the dry sandwich she had made earlier in the day to quieten her growling stomach.

By 17.05 Elizabeth was dressed in the warm clothing she kept in the bag with shoulder straps, hidden in the alleyway of number 45. She would miss her kind neighbour. Lacing new trainers with stiffening fingers she rose and brushed herself down, crumbs falling from the hand-knitted wool.

From the bag she took out the orange purse with the sixty-two pounds in it, and the train ticket to Greenwich paid for by her sister. A single. Elizabeth supposed that she was, now, and she set off up the darkening street.

Granda's Plan
Sherry Morris

Granda died in his armchair, with a tartan blanket over his legs and a book on his lap, while listening to Radio nah Gaidheal in front of the sitting room fire – just as he planned. He must've known his time was coming because earlier in the day he got out the buttons and had me repeat step-by-step what to do with them.

'Keep 'em handy. Don't forget. And make sure you place 'em right,' he instructed while placing the three buttons in my hand, then folding my small fingers over the large circles. They were twice as big as two-pence coins.

'One on each eye. And one on ma mouth.'

As many times as he'd told me, I didn't see how I could forget. I was 10 years old, but I understood things. Especially important things. Like keeping Granda's soul from the faeries.

'Otherwise…,' Granda said, his voice trailing off.

Time and again he'd explained how he needed my help as he couldn't very well do it himself. He couldn't count on his daughter – Mum called his beliefs 'Highland hooey' – Granda said she'd once believed, but that ever since Pop did a runner, she'd had time only for the realities of putting food on the table, clothes on our backs and a roof over our heads. I spent most of my time, even the time I shoulda been in school, with Granda learning the old ways and listening to his stories of the creatures who lived all around us. Granda knew I'd help him, because I believed his stories.

They always started like this:

'Faeries born and bred here in the Highlands match the landscape and the desolation. They're dangerous. Not just moody, downright

15

evil. You don't mess with one, unless you got to,' and he'd tell of Beira the Winter Queen, the hag healer Cailleach, and kelpies. But one evening, he said he had something to show me.

We were sitting in front of the fire. Just him and me. He'd drawn the thick curtains over the windows and doors to keep out the draught – and all the things it carried.

'You're too young to know the story of the wee bairn, but you're old enough to understand the lesson…' he began.

He took three coins out of his pocket. At least I thought they were coins. Copper-coloured, shiny with a date and a face, they were unusual in size, each with a small hole through the middle. He placed them in my hand. I felt their weight.

'Where'd you get these from, Granda?' I asked.

He shrugged.

'How much are they worth?'

'Good question, Calum,' he said, giving me a close look. 'You could say a life.'

Then he told me a new story.

Once there was old man and his daughter gathering the autumn harvest. The daughter had a young son she brought with her to the field and placed on the grass nearby. The morning mist was rising, taking with it the creatures of the night. The child began to cry and whine in an odd way. The daughter went to it, but her father stopped her, saying this was not her child– the faeries had taken it and left an old-man faery in its stead. If they touched this crying creature, they'd never get the child back. Returning to their work in silence, they ignored the cries.

Dusk arrived: the time of the faeries. The old man, who was experienced in these matters and possessed the faculty of second sight, took three coins from his pocket, jingling them while chanting old words. He dropped them in the pocket of the crying faery man-child. Coins such as these brought great favour with the Winter Queen. More favour than a child. The faeries emerged with the child, exchanging it for the man-faery and coins. Safely back home

16

with the child, the grandfather explained he'd tricked the faeries. He hadn't given them coins, but buttons that looked like the ones coveted by their queen. So that they should not attempt to steal the child a second time, the grandfather had the daughter sew similar buttons onto the child's blanket 'til he grew too old to be carried away.

Granda fell silent. There was only the sound of the fire and the wind.

'I was the bairn you saved,' I said, staring at the button coins in my hand.

'Aye,' Granda said. 'And worth each precious penny, no matter the torment they've planned for me in the afterlife. But they'll mind these last three buttons. Just put 'em like I told you – on ma eyes and mouth – and I'll rest in peace.'

I closed my hands around the buttons, but Granda said he'd keep them 'til it was time. I asked how the faeries would torment him, but all he said was, 'That's not fit for young ears. I saw it in m'dreams. Don't want you to.'

Then we went through the plan again.

The evening passed as usual. Mum had already gone to bed, leaving Granda listening to the radio while I read in the sitting room. Before turning in, I put more wood on and said good night. His hug seemed a little tighter and longer than usual.

On Sunday morning, we found him in the chair, his head slumped to one side, still wearing his glasses with a book open on his lap. Granda couldn't have read by the faint light of the fire – which had gone out – but I understood the book's purpose. I studied his face. He looked peaceful – his decoy had worked. Now it was my turn. I insisted on being with him at all times, watching while Mum and Aunt Jenny washed him, dressed him in his best, then laid him out for folk to say their goodbyes. Mum said we had to put him to rest before the ground got hard, setting the burial for the next day. I'd place the buttons on

Granda just before closing the coffin at Dusk.

The last of Granda's friends, Drouth Tommy, offered to sit with me. Granda'd known Tommy'd be useless putting the buttons in place as bad as his shakes were, but he could offer support. Mum had agreed to me having time alone with Granda to say goodbye and went off to chat with guests in the kitchen.

It was only four o'clock, but the light was fading. Dusk was coming – along with all the things it brings. We'd drawn the curtains and Drouth Tommy stood at the door, though what he'd do if something appeared was unclear. We both knew closed curtains and guarded doors didn't stop faeries. I could hear the murmur of guests in the next room, but I also heard the wind. It had picked up and rattled the windows. I looked at Drouth Tommy. His hands were shaking even more than usual. I heard a scritch-scratch coming from the corner near the window, as if a mouse or a bird was in the room.

'Be quick Calum,' Drouth Tommy said. 'I'm afeart!'

My own heart was thumping in my chest and my mouth was dry. My hands shook like Drouth Tommy's, but calmed once I reached into my pocket and felt the smooth coolness of the buttons. I did like I'd been told. One on each eye and the third on Granda's mouth.

'Thanks Granda,' I croaked. My throat was tight. I realised I might cry. I'd been so caught up in my task, the urgency, I'd barely had time to register Granda's passing. The person I loved most in the world had left me. I could feel tears starting. But then movement caught my eye. The light in the room changed. Shadows from the corners began to grow longer and creep towards me. I hurriedly kissed Granda on his forehead. Drouth Tommy helped me close the lid. I felt something brush past my legs, saw a dark blur with gleaming eyes, heard a hiss. Maybe a cat got in? Stepping back, I thought I felt a touch flicker across the back of my neck, like a whisker or a claw. I heard the whisper of a threat and shivered. Goose bumps appeared on my arm. The curtains rustled and a gust of wind swept through the room. Then Mum appeared in the doorway with men to carry away the coffin. I began to relax. I'd completed the task. I'd saved Granda.

But then I wondered: What if the faeries had seen me put the buttons on Granda? Would they now be after me? I had no more buttons. I'd saved him, but who'd save me? The wind answered with a malevolent howl as dusk descended into darkness.

In-Between Dog
Pippa Gladhill

Patrick brought home a giant dog. It came padding into the kitchen after him, all grey and whiskery, with yellow eyes and big teeth glinting in a grin.

'Holy crap –' Dad shrieked. He was in the middle of straining the pasta and dropped the saucepan, clattering into the sink. Pasta spilled everywhere. 'Shit shit shit.' He began scooping it up with his bare hands, plonking it back into the pan.

Patrick said, 'This is Loopy.'

'Loopy?'

'They said it's best to keep the same name.'

'What's it doing here?'

'Isn't he gorgeous?'

'It looks deranged.'

'And I'll take care of him,' Patrick said.

Patrick's away on the oil rig two weeks in every four, so I knew this wasn't a solid way to persuade Dad. But Patrick added quickly 'And Alice can walk him when I'm not here, can't you Alice?'

He didn't look at me when he said this, just did that eye contact thing with Dad. At the same moment Loopy rolled onto his back, paddling his big paws in the air, his tongue lolling out, watching Dad out of the corner of his eye, like *I'm so cute, come and stroke me*, and Dad stopped rescuing the pasta and went over to Loopy, who nuzzled his hand and when we sat down to eat I sneaked Loopy bits of pasta under the table. And that's how Loopy came to live with us.

We'd started French lessons at school. Already I knew all the numbers up to twenty, and we were doing the verb *être* – to be, as in *I am, you are, he is*. Who are you? *Je suis Alice*. Mrs Dent has taught us funny French sayings as well like *Chacun a sa façon de tuer les puces*. This means we all have our unique way of doing things, Mrs Dent explained. Another one she told us was *entre chien et loup*, which in English means *between a dog and a wolf*.

'What do you understand by this?' Mrs Dent asked. No one had a clue. So she said it was the French way of describing that time of day when the light has faded, but it hasn't quite turned into night and it's neither one thing nor the other. It's that in-between time.

So when I took Loopy to the park after school, I taught him some French because, if we go and live in France like Dad and Patrick talked about once, then he will need to understand French as well as English.

'You are a *chien*,' I told him. '*Tu es un chien*.' He cocked his head to one side and watched me. 'Who am I? *Je suis Alice*. Got that Loop?' What he really wanted was for me to throw his slimy blue ball. I didn't know the French word for 'fetch' but I didn't have to tell him in English, or French, because when I chucked the ball as far and hard as I could, he went after it like I've never seen another dog go, so fast and without effort, like he could keep running for ever.

It was meant to be exciting, starting secondary school and walking there by myself. You went past the houses, along the main road, crossed at the lights, left into Worcester Road, past Hill View Road, along for a bit more and then school was there on the right. But one morning two big boys stood waiting at the corner, and when they saw me coming they crossed over the road directly towards me, like they were going to be friendly, but instead they followed behind me. They started shouting hateful, stupid things, about Dad and Patrick. I put my headphones on and walked fast to try to get away from them into school.

They followed me every morning saying these things. Words I didn't want Dad and Patrick to know about.

One day we will go and live in France.

Who am I? *Je suis Alice.* I have a *chien* called Loopy.

He was only allowed off his lead in the park, and he always came back when I called him. We stayed in the park for hours, I threw the ball, he ran, I threw the ball, he ran. And when the light started to go all smudgy and the trees darkened, Loopy turned greyer and smarter than during daytime. He became who he really was, in this in-between time, in the park.

Dad was in the kitchen getting my lunch box together.

'You should be doing this yourself,' Dad said.

'I know, but I'm late.'

'Cheese or ham?'

'Ham, please.'

He checked in the fridge and found there was none. 'It'll have to be cheese.'

'Can I take Loopy to school with me this morning?'

'No.'

'Dad, can we move to France soon?'

He stopped wrapping the greaseproof paper round the sandwich and looked at me, 'Why?'

I shrugged. 'Just asking.'

'We will, one day, hopefully. Now, come on, you'd best hurry.' He handed me my lunch box.

I went and got my coat and let myself out the front door. I banged it shut loudly so Dad would hear and know that I'd left. Dad would be going to shower and get dressed. He wouldn't see me standing there outside the front door, waiting for the last possible minute to leave. Hoping the boys would have given up waiting for me.

I put dog biscuits in my pocket and in the park I taught Loopy to sit. 'Sit,' I told him and pushed his backside down. Then I took a biscuit from my pocket and gave it to him. He got the idea. Then I taught it to him in French. '*Assis*, Loops.' He sat and watched my biscuit pocket closely with his yellow eyes. 'Loopy you are a rare bilingual dog. You understand everything.' He did that mad, happy dog grin. Then we ran about and I played ball with him. In the park was best. In the park, in that in-between time, when Loops became who he really was.

Next day after school I took to Loopy to the park and we waited until the light was all smudgy and the trees were all dark and Loops' eyes burned bright, and then I whispered into his ear. 'Go, Loops,' I said, 'go and eat the boys'. Then I said it in French as well, just in case, as Loops is a bilingual dog. '*Va manger les garçons.*' He loped away, head down, a grey shadow, past the trees and out of the park.

I went home. Dad was in the kitchen making soup and doing a crossword.

'Two down, *be thorough over a task*,' he said.

'How many letters?'

'Four, five. Where's Loopy?' he said.

'He's gone to eat the boys,' I said.

'Really?' said Dad, filling in the answer and not listening properly.

'Yuh. Really.'

There was a thud at the front door. I went to open it and Loops came in, all grey and bristled, with an excited air about him, bringing a blast of the cold night with him.

'Hey, Loops,' I said, 'have a biscuit,' and I took one from my pocket and gave it to him, but for once he wasn't hungry.

I never saw those two big boys again. And we haven't moved

to France yet. But I'm teaching Loopy more French words for when we do. We go to the park every day after school, where Loops runs about as the light fades to that in-between moment when it's neither one thing or the other, and Loops becomes more who he really is, and I'm glad Dad and Patrick never got to hear those stupid words about them.

Who am I? I am Alice. *Je suis Alice* and my friend is a *chien* called Loopy.

They Said there were Pirates
Kirsty Fox

A memory, or a dream. Something slipping from the seas of my subconscious as I hold my mother's hand and clasp a coin into her lined palm. She's older now. So am I and our minds drift.

They said there were pirates on the seas. I didn't believe them. But lying in the belly of the boat, listening to the shift and creak of battered wood, I began to believe. They told me to leave behind any treasure. That they would keep it safe. But I kept the old coin my brother gave me, smooth and brave in my palm when I reached into my pocket to check for it.

Mama had laughed when I told her what the other kids said about pirates. A bright laugh to chase away the bad.

'You're my only treasure,' she said. 'I have nothing left to lose.'

She didn't know about the coin my little brother gave me.

It was black at sea. A deep blackness barely bitten by the sliver of a half moon which peeked from somewhere in the ocean of clouds that rested on the ocean of water. There was an oil lamp on the boat somewhere between silhouetted figures. Earlier, when I'd been sat up on Mama's knee, I could see this light pick out the creep of close waves and the red tint on faces in the dusk. But beyond this tiny light there was mostly blackness. So now I'd made a cabin for myself, wriggling beneath the benches and feet, down into the belly of the boat. I was not as small as my brother, but still small enough to hide like an animal. To become invisible for when the pirates came.

The boat was slick with sweat from the long day exposed to a hazy sun. But now the sweat was cold and clammy. I sensed something was coming. Even though the night was silent save for the lap of waves, and the boat was silent save for cramped passengers shifting uneasily. Some of them on the edge were clinging on, for even though the sea was quiet now, rogue waves had already stolen from our human cargo.

I could tell Mama thought I was asleep. Her body, which hovered above on the bench I used as my cabin roof, had relaxed slightly. She hadn't really slept since the day we left home. Since the day we cradled my dead brother amid the bloodshed. Since she gave up hope that Grandpa would return.

I'd been part of the water for so long it no longer felt like I was moving. The rumble of my stomach swayed inside me, but I was still. We were still. Only the creak and shift of the battered wooden boat told me we weren't still. As though it was the planet that swayed to and fro. To and fro. While I stayed still and waited for the pirates to come.

Yes, Twilight
Math Jones

The twilight of the gods, the Ragnarok, is presaged by the death of Baldur. Frigg, his mother, gains the promise of all things to do Baldur no harm. Cunning Loki tricks the blind god Hodr into killing Baldur with an arrow of mistletoe, the only thing not to swear. Frigg's revenge is terrible. Loki is bound, with a venom-dripping serpent set over his head. Earth tremors are his writhings. The twilight of the gods, the Ragnarok, will follow on Loki's release.

The earth is quaking as we get there.

Splintered giant-bone shivering like a spear-hit, threatens, louring dead-etin, to fall, to drag giant-skull from dwarven hands.

There is a steam-splash of venom flung aside onto rock, cry of steps upon the dust, then the screaming and the shaking stops.

He lies quiet again, on the boulders we bound him to, with the entrails of his children still calling, Father, Father.

His wife is kneeling, blister-fingered, armed with agony, the bowl, still smoking, held now above his head as shield.

Above his head too, the spitting serpent. Drip, drip, drip, smoking venom's caught.

His face smoking too.

My husband takes his place, sits himself by Loki's head. Grim blue against the blue stone. Takes a breath that includes spittle-snake, mountain-musk, settling dust, and blood-brother. My husband runes.

I tie my own gaze to Loki's wife. Sigyn does not speak, but allows me to take the bowl of glowing acid, kneels again, singing to remake her husband's face.

As smoke clears, head hung between their galdr, an eye emerges from the seething skin. Our spouses' songs enter the holes, each side of Loki's skull. Echo in his thought. His eye gains its target.

With a gurgle and his own spit of heated-water, Loki tries to speak. It is like when his mouth was stitched, but not so comical. He is hushed by wife and brother, learns to listen again.

My husband runes.

I can hear the thrum of Loki's children in the guts binding him. I helped rip them myself. They sound starkly alive in the dead-silence of my own son. In the dead-emptiness of my own son in that moment.

When my son hollowed out, when Baldur was a fresh weight again in my arms. When he fell but did not rise. That moment the littlest plant slivered into him, stopped his heart. That moment, thrown by a blind brother, guided by this one's spite. Despite. In spite of...

The venom growing heavy in my arms now.

My son and son's-wife lying on the burning ship, clasping a gold-dripping ring. Fire on the twilight sky. Sleipnir leaping the walls, the fire-walls, of Hel. Sleipnir leaping again. Walking the worlds again, collecting tears from all that had kept their promises, finding mistletoe already weeping. Only this one, Loki, dry-eyed, fire-eyed, and worse, dressed as a woman.

Fire-venom growing earth-heavy now, grief-heavy.

My husband runes.

Earth is still, with my arms protecting still the face of my child's killer.

Sun and Moon are still too. Day and Night are still too. Their wagons have not rolled since he died. No. I got their promises at twilight. Along with all the things within the world. Not to hurt my son. Night promised not to fall. Day promised to stay bright. Sun promised not to burn. Moon not to wane. Only mistletoe, too young –

It was as if we all held our breath.

Sun and Moon, Day and Night holding still. And the wolves still coming.

But if you had heard him. If you had heard him crying in his nightmare, the fracture of his most naked fear, crying for his mother no longer there – always slender-willed, my son, his golden-light bare to sing or scream...

Still the wolves are closing in.

My husband runed to me a tale in our bed, his hand unwelcome on my breast. But I took it anyway.

The tale-bearing witch he had loved is dead, her voice unwelcome in her own head.

Would I know more, or what? Yes.

A tale of burning, yes. Thunder poisoned by the snake's breath, splitting its skull with his fall. The Listener and this one drowned in each other's arms. My husband lying dead in the bile of a wolf's gut. Yes.

But, a tale of returning too. Life and Lust-for-Life emerging from the scorched tree. Magni, Modhi, Thrud, hammer in their hands. Fields growing of themselves. Sun's daughter rousing her young horses to ride a new day. My son gathering up the scattered playing-pieces in the grass. Yes.

My husband runes: year and the tree: yes.

The blistered skull spits. Yes.

His wife. Yes.

My husband lifts his spear. The snake leaves its place, coils down the shaft, my husband's arm. I tip the venom away.

Together, Loki's wife and I, weavers both, unbind her children.

Last drop of bitterness.

Outside, it is dusk, still. Sun and Moon, Day and Night are holding still, keeping promises. We wave them back onto their roads. The wolves are close.

Loki and Sigyn go swiftly. Odin and I remain, together in the twilight.

Wolf's Head
Penny Pepper

Once wrapped in his fur, the wolf spread his juice upon me. I stand in the grove and look at my hands as the light of day bleeds away. Am I cursed? Do I care?

There is a wet jewel of blood, a slow dribble falling between my breasts. A few scratches and nips.

I watch him lope away. He says he'll call me back soon, words he likes, words that spellbind me. I can't move. His shape fades into the thick growing twilight. Owls rustle, cats blink. I don't want him to leave.

He says he has duties, that he must warrior his way around his domain.

I lift my hands and smell them, soaking up his odour.

In the distance, I see him – he's stopped. His sharp outline glows with the unfocused blur of rising moonlight. I freeze, wondering what he's thinking.

He told me I didn't have to. I was young, he said. Not so young, I replied, grabbing him, tugging his paws into my secret places. There was frenzy within me, a hunger that made me howl. I'm hungry, flesh and blood I yelped, brushing my face into his hair as his scents seeped into my marrow.

He's too far away now for me to see if he's moving. I wonder what ticks and tricks through his mind.

The days are long. I climb a thousand stairs to get to the top of a tower where I live. It seethes with bad odours and gives home to large defiant rats. Children smoke strange substances, tormenting each other with knives. There is often dried blood on the concrete steps, hardened stinking shit and suspicious rags curled into tortured flesh bundles that no-one owns.

Through my glass window I stare at the siren moon and ache to be released to him, to flee into the distant forest. A thousand steps below, the other world exists. Its noise and its clawing, its lost people, tied to burdens and tasks, and tiny aimless hopes. I was one of them once, a time ago, before the wolf claimed me with his glare and his intangible commandments to follow.

At least I can see the sky. In the corner, grandmother rocks towards the shattered wall. She rolls in a skein of wool and a thousand spiders come out to unwind it, before her hands begin again. In a soft voice she crows, pulling it back, speaking in tongues of fractured memory. Tells the air secrets, whispers to the ghosts of fate and danger. Her eyes look to me and she always cries.

I hear him in a dream and bathe myself before I go to his call. I dress plainly in a velvet coat. Grandma puts a winter violet in my hair and a pomegranate in my hands, murmuring to beware the seeds.

Near the bottom of the steps an old man leans against the angry concrete. His beard knots in snarls of dirt and grey. I did not catch his gaze but as I move, he grabs my wrist, his bone fingers scarring my skin.

He chants. 'Don't give yourself to the likes of him. Those sorts ruin you. Take you, eat you. He's done it to many. Don't give yourself to the likes of him.'

'Leave me alone,' I cry as I wrench from his fear and his aging flesh. 'You just want to hunt him because he is wild and different, because he frightens you.'

'Yes, he frightens me. He should frighten you. His kind cause nothing but hurt and destruction, and take us to places we should not go.'

'You don't know him like I do.' I smile as I run, not looking back. 'He won't harm me.'

I run and I run, and the other world flees. The dirt and the noise, the machines in motion, the frenetic petty actions of those strayed from the old path, where they once belonged with the wolf and the owl, the bird and the fox, the oak and the yew.

I skip into the forest and dance with my love. He rolls me around, pricks his ears, growls out love and desire. His teeth are sharp but I cry in pleasure. He mounts me and the pomegranate splits into slick fragments, the violet crushes from my hair.

The moon shivers and turns red. I howl. I roll my eyes to the stars. My love looks at me, his ears down.

I do not know myself as I roar. Teeth snap from my mouth with a deadly cut. Into his throat I bite, and I bite. He yelps softly and I see the sad, accepting glow in his eyes.

My coat is thick with his blood, I shake it, swing it back onto on my shoulders.

A while later I race deeper into the woods.

Over my head, a proud trophy, and one of love. There he is, his fine pelt hanging over my shoulders, his ears pert, his eyes staring, forever staring. We are one now, always.

I draw back my lips.

It is time to howl, it is time to smile and time to call out for another.

Flick'ring Shadows
David Mathews

'Good evening, ladies and gentlemen. Welcome to the gallery and to pictures by one of our favourite photographers. Smith is sorry that he can't be here himself, but he has asked me, as the show's curator, to introduce you to a few of these 'low lights', portraits and scenes he has shot after sunset, mostly outdoors, all without flash.

'So, if you'll follow me, I'll introduce you to my personal favourites.

'My number one is also Smith's choice. A schoolgirl, seen as she wished to be, looking straight at the camera, slight pout, ribbons loose in her fair hair, tie half way round her neck. Not, you guess, how her mother envisaged her portrait. And notice the light: pale pink sky above the trees graduating to the deep blue of evening higher up. The face with barely a shadow, but it's lit enough to show freckles.'

Josie age 7, November 2009. C-print

Josie came to my studio with her mother, after school. She knew her mind. She arrived at my door on her bike, mum trailing, and asked me right away if we could do the shoot outside.

'In the park or by the river?' I said.

'Ooh, by the river.'

Josie wanted to look like a gypsy. Which bit of being a gypsy, I needed to know. She showed me her best sultry, brooding look. Mother frowned, but I laughed, and Josie did a sulk so profound that it might have been the best picture I never took.

Trouble was, the light was going. We were meant to be in the studio, not beside the river, ducking bats as they chased their supper. I suggested we let the dark do the gypsy thing, and Josie got my drift. She was great. We played tricks in the half light.

A magazine bought two shots, and my phone went berserk.

I wish I had had a daughter. I never quite managed that.

'Here we have Smith, by himself. Yesterday I went to see him in hospital. He's doing OK. He's lost a bit of weight since he took this picture five years ago, but even here he's long and lean. He describes himself as an apprentice wraith, and he certainly looks like he's not seen sunlight for a while, for all that he's dark skinned. But not many ghosts wear specs.'

Self-portrait, 2011. Giclée print

I did not plan a self-portrait. I had done a few moody shoots in low light with a clear sky, at the end of what we call the blue hour. I even had a couple where you could see Venus. But what could I make of an overcast sky after sunset? I took the tripod outside, and was going to ask passers-by if I could shoot them, when my neighbour who runs the takeaway said that if I did some pictures of him, he would do me. I set up the shot. He said, 'Left a bit – no I meant right, my left,' and pressed the button. Strictly speaking, this is not a self-portrait at all.

'I puzzled over this picture for an hour. What do you think that is top left, a bat? It's scarcely more than a blur. And to the right, out of shot, must be a streetlamp, and somebody making the shadow that takes up half the picture. The river is there, bottom left, but how far away I can't tell, so deceptive is the light. Maybe the elusiveness is the point.'

Just a Song at Twilight, 2012. Giclée print

As well as shooting pictures of people in this intriguing light, I have tried to record the tricks that dusk plays on our visual perception.

'I can't add anything to what Smith says about this next one.'

Women Playing Bowls by Torchlight, 2011. Giclée print from mobile phone.

I have had a fondness for evenings since I was a child. In Port of Spain we would play cricket until it was too dark to see the ball, and even then we would try to carry on by the light from a doorway. I was Gary Sobers. When I came across these beautiful ladies playing bowls in near darkness – they must have all been in their eighties – it took me back to those evenings. Brilliant; except the only thing that really was brilliant was the white jack that Doris was shining her torch on. It was their last outdoor match of the year, and they were going to finish it if it took till midnight. I felt they should be called in for supper.

'A few years ago we hosted a show called Life before Death, 24 pairs of portraits by Walter Schels. In each pair the subject is shown in the days before their death and shortly after they died. It was dignified and uplifting. Sandra, who you see in these two photographs, was much taken with the show, and asked Smith to do the same for her. I think it's fair to say that he did not do it as an obligation, but as an act of love. As you can see from the light in the window behind Sandra's chair, these are evening shots; evening in a figurative sense too.'

Sandra Before and After her Death, 20 and 21 May, 2014. Digital C-print

I did not relish shooting these pictures, but I am privileged to have done them. We never completely made a couple, Sandra and me, but we never completely broke up either. Maybe we should have had our own little Josie (Picture #1). My fault, if fault must be allocated. When Sandra's illness came, and she asked me to photograph her in those last days and after her last breath, I thought it ghoulish. But she talked me round, and it became a joint project to which, you have to say, Sandra contributed more than me.

'This could be a still from a black and white movie, couldn't it? It is colour, but so washed out you barely notice. The stone doorway could be in Palermo or Naples. The man? Slicked hair, designer spectacles, immaculate grey suit, handmade shoes. Half in shadow he seems furtive, not quite legit. But he's not the godfather, more – what do they call them – more the *consigliere*?'

The Cabinet Minister, 2014. Giclée print

I knew him from the papers as a solid technocrat of a minister, not one to inspire a following or rouse an audience. Others, however, had ambitions for him, seeing him as fitted for one of the great offices of state, even PM the election after next, once the tedious referendum was done with. He needed a new look, they thought, needed to be seen in a new light by the public and, especially, party members.

The shoot was appalling. Brian tried hard, but was unable to ignore the camera or to pose to good effect, his face and body unfamiliar to him as tools of politics. I felt desperate for him.

Then the light went. He told me his favourite film was *The Third Man*. It was mine too, so I got him to skulk in a doorway, and shot this. He relaxed then. I was able to do a couple of decent promo shots, but he and I liked this one best. We discovered that we had more in common than movies – but everyone knows that now. The official line was that they needed a cabinet reshuffle, but his sacking was bigotry really. Brian is a lovely man and a dear friend.

'The last picture I want to show you actually is in black and white. A middle-aged woman by a tea and coffee kiosk, the light from which has caught her cigarette smoke. You can barely see anything else. It made Smith nostalgic for his fags, and he gave me this updated text yesterday.'

Bajan Woman in a Park, 2012. Digital C-print

A proper smoker, she was. Should I go for black and white to show off the smoke, or colour to focus on the glow of the ciggie in the gloom? I went for the smoke, for old times' sake as much as anything. Until 10 years ago, I was a fifty a day man. Loved my *Pall Malls*. Enid is holding a *Dunhill*. I miss smoking, and when they told me I had cancer, I wondered why I had bothered to give it up. The hospital told me today that they think they have cut it all out, and that the real benefit from having quit is my heart. My consultant wants me to die of old age, so I asked her, if I make 21 years and get to 80, how would it be if I took up smoking again? She asked me if I was a betting man.

Here
Samuel Wright

Witchcraft here was a thing of bone and gristle, and nails. Thick nails, square headed. On a barn, an owl, wings wide and bloody, nailed to the beam to ward off storms. In the chimney breast, a toad, thick with soot and pinned with thorns. Under the bedstead, behind a brick, a bullock's heart studded with iron.

But here, sheep die, stones fall, nothing changes unless you heave it into place with your own hands. And if you love something you grip it tight.

On a clear day, you could see him in the top field from the village. A speck, moving slowly. His sheep, his dog, his wife. But there weren't many clear days. Mist hung in this valley, and the fields he owned were the last green patches under the scree.

When you could see, you might guess what he was doing. If he was still, hunched by the wall, he was replacing tumbled stones. If you watched you would feel it in your own rough hands. The grit on palms. The weight tested, the dirt brushed. The grut and scrape, a sharp push with the heel of the hand. Leaning, pulling, feeling the pieces lock together. Everyone built walls, with stones piled generations back and then placed and replaced year by year.

If he moved, an energetic bend to his back, his wife beside him in a corner of the field, he was digging the earth dry. And when you watched that you too felt the freezing mud, the cold blade of the adze, the trickle as the drain began to flow and the drenched field began to release the load of water that rolled down hills and caught in the folds and hollows and bred flies and sickness in the flock.

And if he cornered a sheep, and bent over it, he might be doing many things. He might be holding the bucking head with a knee against the neck, feeling the horns scraping against the stone wall, gripping the oily wool and pulling up a hoof to dig the rot out. He might be pulling a dazed animal up, trying to make it stand as sickness staggered and blinded it. He might be turning it to see the pink, distended uterus that hung down, torn by panicked hooves. And then he might be taking out his knife to slit its throat and let it bleed out on the mud before he slung it on his shoulders to carry home.

When you watched that, you smelt the oil on your fingers and the blood under your nails, and you knew, as everyone does here, that the things we know are the things we can hold.

A farmer's wedding is a thing of coarse jokes and slapped arses. When you breed sheep, you need sons, and sentimentality is for those who don't have to hold the knife. But love can still come, and come strong. Maybe it is the heart under the bed, or maybe it is the night when some space opens up, for a moment, and you touch without pressing.

Or maybe it just takes some people. People like him, with eyes that puzzle over moss, and a rock loose and rattling in his heart.

She followed him always, beetling across that top field. Early days it was close, so close they sometimes touched, and stopped, while the dog circled them. But stony men are stony men, and it came that she lagged and lagged while he lost the way of her in the mud of his fields. The dog looped further and further. It was a huge, loping animal, more than half wolf, they said.

In those times they still talked of wolves. They were gone, but their memory remained, and it was easy to believe they might remain in the dark on the far side of the old walls. When they talked of them they talked of sheep torn open, children taken, dogs bitten and rabid. On the older farms, when their dogs died they sometimes took a paw and nailed it to the gate of the field, a charm to ward off the wolves that weren't there.

But he said he'd seen them. At auction, after he'd sold his sheep, he'd have a drink at the Bear. He said he heard them at night, and he'd seen their shadows slipping under gates. The others laughed gently, touching him with hard, friendly hands, but he shrank back.

'That dog would see off any wolf,' they said.

When he placed his glass back down, the bottom rattled against the slate bar.

The next auction day the only sheep he brought was dead.

In the village they watched him, hunched, his wife trailing behind. She stopped at the gate, and he walked on down to the village, the carcase across his shoulders. By the time he reached the valley floor the blood from it had pinked his neck, and the smell where his sweat had slicked the butcher's stink of the gut was rank. He threw it down, and part of it fell out of a torn hole in its side.

The village stared.

He turned and walked back.

When he was gone, they touched it with the toes of their boots. The flap of belly skin was ripped in a wide swathe.

He stayed up there for months. All winter they only saw him toiling across the white. His wife trailed further, and his dog circled slowly.

She disappeared in spring. The dog went first, and then her.

He came to the Mayday auction. His eyes slipped back and forth across his face. He had no sheep to sell, but spent the day at the Bear.

'They took the dog,' he said. His voice was shivered, a splinter of half sounds.

One of the old men drew near. 'Wolves?'

He nodded. His hands held the glass. Long scratches ran down the back of them.

'Or men?'

He looked up. The old man had aged past all expression, but his eyes were sharp. There was enough animal in everyone round here to believe that shapes might shift, and natures turn in the dark.

'Do you have the body?'

He nodded.

'Take the paw.'

If you had watched, you might have seen him hammer something to a gate high on the stony back of the hill.

When the men of the village were boys, the tales of wolves had been more than just lost sheep. They had heard the cries at night, the howl that sounded half human, at least to an ear primed to hear it. Full moons, bright nights where a girl might grunt against a back wall and the hand that held her shoulder had nails that came close to claws. When a kiss was close to a punch, and you carried a dead lamb like a wet sack, the thought of turning fully, of being the wolf that most were halfway towards was not so strange.

Everyone here knew the taste of blood, and the thinness of skin.

So when he came down one last time and said that it had changed, there was enough to make five men go. They walked in the half-light to the gate in the high field where he'd nailed the dog's paw.

In June, the hills still held cold glimmers of sun past ten o'clock. At midnight, when they reached it, the rocky crest of the hill was a blue grey shadow against a lighter sky. And yes, the moon was full and round.

He walked with them, stiff and strange. His eyes were fixed now. He'd looked mad before, but now he just looked afraid.

He stopped twenty yards back. They could see where he'd nailed it. It had been there for weeks now, but the air was still cold this high up, and there was enough left to see that it was no dog's paw.

The five stepped closer to look. The nail was struck neatly through the palm. One drew back, but the others looked closer. Sometimes you found a sheep in a crevice, higher than this, and rather than rotting away, the skin would dry over the bone, pulling back to reveal teeth, hardening and blackening into leather. This hand had dried, into the thinnest of black gloves. The wrist bone beneath shone white. A gold wedding band sparkled loosely at the base of the ring finger.

And now they all drew back. They looked at him. He touched the long scratches that ran down the backs of his wrists.

The rest of her was in the kennel, thin, dead. They hanged him in the autumn.

Words on Paper
Rob Walton

I know some things.

I know about Fibonacci and nature. I know if I pick the petals from the sunflowers I grow in my garden I will count 34. I know, therefore, if I chant 'He loves me, he loves me not, he loves me...' it will end in disappointment. I know sunflowers can have 55 or 89 petals. I know I can engineer the answers. I know if I stare at the last of the sunflowers at dusk I bring more light into my day.

I know there's a difference between 800g lining paper and 1200g lining paper, especially when you're writing poems on it. Poems about a person you may or may not love, about a person you want to love, about a person who may or may not love you, poems as advertisements. The grade and weight matter when you're pasting these poems on paper to the windows of your local shop.

I know a row of shops with a butcher, a baker and a mischief-maker. Mrs Mehra has always been up for anything, especially mischief. It perhaps wasn't what you'd expect of her when you saw her but, as Denzil says, never judge a book by its cover. Alice, who was staying with me, says *Never judge an app by its logo*. This annoys me more than it should. It makes me want to pour her Ricard in her bag or smash the bottle against her bedroom wall, until I remember that it's my bedroom wall. Every night out she takes a bottle of Ricard in her bag. She's too poor for some things, but she's never too poor for Ricard. That could be her epitaph: *Let no-one doubt that she was ne'er too poor for Ricard.* (I could write it in that red Sharpie she's always carrying with her. When you ask her why she's got it, she taps her nose and winks.) Alice is too poor to fix her iPad that is still covered in an eating and drinking accident from last Christmas. I'm told that's really bad for them. She'd been ill as she was getting into bed, and wiped it with her Secret Santa Minnie Mouse slipper. She came back to my place at New Year and said she was going to get it sorted on her credit card. Her new credit card where her name was spelt differently: *Mr R. Ellis*. I thought she probably had the card for effect. I never saw her use it. Alice was kind of flaky and kind of alluring. Sometimes me and Denzil argued about which it was, but we kept switching sides.

I know I'm jumpy. Forgive me.

Our mischief-maker wears a black suit, and she sells pretty much everything. She even has a bucket to mix the wallpaper paste, and she has the paste. Who buys this stuff with their groceries? The bucket and the paste are the things I had forgotten. I didn't have that much to remember, it wasn't an overly complex procedure. Once I'd made the decision to go for the 800g grade, for what Denzil kept referring to as *ease of application and adhesion*, it should have been straightforward.

I was listening to Frankie and the Heartstrings' *Hunger* on a huge black CD player Mrs Mehra dragged out front, which wasn't perhaps my brightest idea. It's music that's great for lots of things – hearing live, in the car sometimes, in the house, in clubs, especially at festivals – but as a sensible accompaniment to putting up wallpaper it's down there with drinking super strength lager through a straw. Fun? Yes. Helpful? No. There'd be some steady bits where I'd get a real rhythm with the paste brush but there's that bit at the end of *It's Obvious* which led to a few rips and *Don't Look Surprised* made me break the pasting table. I had to improvise on the pavement, which led to words being smudged, erased, and somehow scratched. Words being scratched or smudged I quite liked. I wasn't so keen on them being erased.

This verse stuff had taken a lot of time. I don't sleep so well when the clocks change. There'd been lots of disturbed nights reaching for the phone to record ideas, or getting a cheap biro to make a note on a music magazine from last year that now lived next to my bed. On the tissue box there was an almost-brilliant rhyme that I was about to forget about. It would soon be remembered and light up one of my evenings.

I covered the shop windows with the words on paper. All of them. Mrs Mehra went along and told me if I'd missed a bit. I don't know what she was getting out of this, but I knew I'd never buy my buckets anywhere else. If things went well I might even buy one for Alice's bedside.

When there was no glass to be seen, I waited for the reaction. Mixed is the word people use in such circumstances. Some people were slightly afraid and some were unhappy. Mr Crump, grubby and grumpy butcher, turned round and went back to his shop without speaking or showing any emotion. Denzil's brother said,

'I don't want to see poetry. I want to see Mrs Mehra's special offers. I want to look through the window and see that tray with no samosas. Now look. It's like something out of a black and white European film you've recommended. One I won't watch until the end.'

At lunchtime there was more interest. People were taking photos. There was a spate of selfies. I couldn't work out if this was a good thing. I was hoping someone would come with a Box Brownie, or a sketch pad or a notebook. I wanted it to be this event thing. I wanted slow art. It wasn't going to happen.

At quarter past one it all changed. This boy came and he looked good. He looked really good. I – let's be clear about this – I liked the look of this boy. It was becoming.

Then I thought I recognised him. Was he a friend of Alice's? I'd seen him – or I thought I had, I'm not sure how reliable a narrator I am, I'm jumpy, remember – but, yes, I thought I might have seen him in the old independent cinema at the top of the bank. *The Bicycle Thieves* was on – which, I suppose, in a way is where the idea for this came from. Or at least it was a thought or an image which met something else floating around my head and then moved on to the idea to do this – what to call it? Flyposting? Poemposting? So, The Bicycle Thieves – you really must see it. Don't listen to Denzil's brother. I'm not usually a recommender, or if I am I'll be very inarticulate – but it's a film to see. The man, the protagonist, goes out on his bicycle to paste posters on billboards and his bike is stolen. The pasting struck me – and at the same time I had this idea for a killer poem – I can, sometimes, stand outside all this and be objective – and realised I had to take things in my own hands.

I read this review of the film which spoke of a man riding high in the morning and being brought down by night-time. Only he's not. It ends at dusk and he's holding his little boy's hand, looking ahead at the big city. There's a tiny bit of light between their palms, and sometimes that's enough.

It was like the poem as an advertisement had worked. The good-looking boy could be my ally in all this. Maybe he already was. He was there at the genesis, and so I told him about the next stage and he didn't run away.

I'd been thinking of it as Speakers' Corner, but it was just me at the top of the bank reading the poem out loud. He sat near my feet, looked at me and listened. Mrs Mehra and Denzil looked up, shielding their eyes from something. I thought I saw Alice (who spoke of *Ladri di biciclette*) coming out of the shop with a bottle of Ricard. She was with Denzil's brother. They were raising a toast to lingering light and developing love.

So my poems stayed on lining paper on Mrs. Mehra's shop windows for the rest of the week and I was happy. A local arts magazine got a photographer there, and I got the boy and the others to stand near me and we all put our arms round each other. I think that was one of the things I wanted.

Things moved on. Alice moved away. I bought her a bucket and we kissed and hugged. The lovely boy eventually departed.

He actually rode a bicycle into the sunset – but not before he moved in to my flat, taking Alice's place. He always arrived at dusk, after work or college or whatever he did. I never asked. We spent evening after evening dancing and kissing as we shared our Frankie and the Heartstrings young love soundtrack.

We papered the windows in the flat and wrote stuff down, our story. Eventually we blocked out too much of the light, so we could only see ourselves and it stopped being enough.

I sometimes use the red Sharpie I stole from Alice to add bits to the story, and then I dance a bit more. It's all I know.

One Two Three, One Two Three
Rosalind Stopps

This is how I know that timing is important.

My mother was a formation dancer.

'Timing is everything,' she said. 'Count it out and you can make order out of chaos, keep the dark at bay. If you keep counting your life will be a dance. Mess up the steps a little? You can get the order back, just as long as you never miss a beat. Remember that.'

I saw the chaos around me and I started to count. My mother knew that if her timing had been more accurate I would never have been conceived.

'We were backstage at the Tower Ballroom in Blackpool,' she said, 'and I thought we wouldn't have time to go all the way, but the team from Hong Kong had a mishap. The call was ten minutes late and by then you were on the way.'

'I kept dancing when I was pregnant,' she used to tell me, 'right up to the end and then again six weeks after. I was better on the slow ones but I never sat out a quickstep even though they asked me to.'

Hearing this story when I was a little boy I used to think that they had asked her to sit it out because of concern for her and even for me, jigging around in her belly like a kitten in a washing machine.

'I loved the Paso Doble,' she said, 'my favourite.'

She would fling anything round her shoulders when she said this, a coat, a dishcloth, once a sheet of newspaper. This was the part I liked. The sun was bright.

'Ole!' she shouted and I had to circle her, slowly at first and then more quickly while she turned on her knees following my movements and with her eyes on mine, all the way. I got the slow part, the bullfighter, and as long as I counted and stamped my foot we were dancing, all else forgotten.

This is how I know that there is a down side to timing.

Even at school I counted my steps, one two three, one two three, making sure I paid particularly close attention to detail when chaos loomed. I knew how many steps from the playing field to the hut and I knew how long it would take to get changed and get home. I thought I might be one of the people who are happier when they are older.

'You, boy, is football a joke?' the teacher shouted. I had taken my eye off the ball and I had got to two thousand and thirty six, with home time not far away.

'No sir,' I said.

'No sir?' he bellowed as if it was the most ridiculous thing he had ever heard. 'No sir? It's not a joke then?'

'No sir,' I said again. I didn't know where this was going but it wasn't going well and I was worried about losing my place in the numbers that determined my life.

'Then why the hell are you smiling?'

'There are three hundred and six steps to the changing room,' I said.

It was the first thing that came into my head but the response was not good. The light dimmed a little. The rest of my school career was spoilt by whispered counting and sniggering from all sides.

This is how I know that timing is a random bastard.

Take falling in love, and choosing a life partner. Picture life as a shooting gallery. At the beginning millions of faces are lined up, but some of them fall down straight away. They are the people you would have met if you had been born in Finland or Rwanda, or too early or too late. Everywhere you go after that, some faces pop up and some fall down and every time you make a choice like, studying chemistry, more faces fall flat, thousands of them. They are the people you might have met if you had learned Spanish or left school to live in Nepal. The rows shuffle every time you walk down a street or eat a bagel and miss your train until finally you're at a party and you've drunk too much to drive home and there she is. The only face that came up in the shooting gallery shuffle for that time and that place and you think, maybe I'll marry her. And in another gallery, millions of faces shuffle forward and back, the millions of children you could have had. It's all part of the dance, and all you can do is to keep on counting and pray to Whoever Keeps the Score that you don't trip up.

'If you trip,' my mother used to say, 'just adjust the count until you're where you should be again, then count on from where you are.'

'How can you know where you should be in the dark?' I want to ask her now, 'and who the hell is keeping the score?'

This is how I know that time is running out.

We met under the clock at Carnforth station. She asked if I could dance and I told her, 'I can dance to your tune if you'll let me'.

'A funny man', she said. 'I like a funny man. Let me tell you this then, funny man, I'm a whore.'

Only after five minutes did I understand that it was a joke. Only after five minutes did she explain that the study of timekeeping is called horology and that was her hobby.

I was hooked.

'That's my kind of joke,' I said and I stopped thinking about all the people I wasn't meeting and all the streets I wasn't going to walk down. There was order again. I forgot the woman I had married when I couldn't count my steps correctly and the children we hadn't had because my sperm had been timed out on their egg hunt. Instead I watched that one face as she bent over her beloved clocks, sorting through parts so tiny and intricate it seemed terrible to hide them away again when the clock was mended. She laughed when I told her that, and made me a clock with every little spring on show. I keep it by the bed and I watch it when she is sleeping. The tick keeps coming while I try not to think of how much longer we could have had.

One – two – three, one – two – three. Never miss a beat.

'It's not the amount of time we have that's important,' she said, 'it's what we do with it.'

So we've seen the northern lights together and we've travelled on trains across time zones and fields of snow. We've looked down from the Shard and up to the stars and we've eaten on the beach while the water lapped at our feet.

I have been too happy to keep time and still I don't think that I ever missed a step but what I know now is this – time keeps itself. Even if you stop counting.

'Not long now, darling,' she says, as if she is keeping me from some important engagement.

'The longer the better,' I say but she looks at me in that way she has that means, come on, no need to say anything.

'It's dusk,' she says, 'the light is going.'

It's early in the day but she's right, the light is going.

'Do that bull fighting dance,' she says.

'My timing is not good today,' I tell her and she laughs although it is not funny. And because she laughs and because I am grateful to her for laughing I put the red towel from the bathroom round my shoulders and I hum along to 'Thriller' while I step out to the count and she moves a little, from side to side and I feel the chaos approaching with the dusk and I think

this is how I know that timing cannot always keep the chaos away.

Daylight Savings
David Hartley

Sam: It's your Dad.

Jenny: Hold on a sec.

Sam: He says are you turning the clocks back?

Jenny: Just doing it!

Sam: She's just doing it John. Yeah. Say that again?

Jenny: I'm doing it now Dad! What's the time?

Sam: He says to keep turning it. I don't know what he's on about, here.

Jenny: Hiya Dad.

John: Hello pet. Are you turning the clock back?

Jenny: Just doing it now.

John: Right well don't stop. Keep turning it.

Jenny: You what?

John: Don't stop at one hour, keep going! Turn it slowly though, take it slow.

Jenny: What you on about? Sam, what's the time?

John: Keep turning, keep going!

Sam: 10:04. No, 10:05. It's dark out. Streetlights are still on. Is that right?

Jenny: 10:05.

John: Keep turning Jenny! Trust me pet. Keep going back. Slowly; an hour every thirty seconds.

Jenny: Dad what are you on about? It only goes back one hour.

Sam: Is he alright?

Jenny: Dunno.

John: We're doing it, we're all doing it!

Jenny: Are you outside somewhere Dad? You sound like you're outside. Where are you?

John: Are you still turning it?

Jenny: No.

John: Turn it Jenny!

Jenny: Ok, alright, I'm turning it.

Sam: What's going on?

John: Take it slow. One hour every thirty seconds or so.

Jenny: He says to keep turning it.

John: Put me on speaker, love.

Jenny: Put it on speaker.

Sam: What's all this, John?

John: Hello again, Sam. Just trust me. Tell our Jenny to keep turning the clock.

Jenny: I am Dad.

Sam: She is.

Jenny: How long for?

John: Just keep going!

Jenny: Where are you Dad? Are you outside? You'll catch your death. Is it raining?

John: Don't worry about me, pet. Just make sure you keep turning the clock. One hour every thirty –

Jenny: Yeah, yeah every thirty seconds, I've got it.

John: Is little Sarah there? You there Sarah?

Jenny: No, she's downstairs.

John: Fetch her up; she's got to see this. This is wonderful, magical.

Jenny: Dad, I don't understand…

John: What you on now? What time?

Jenny: Just coming up to two.

John: Great, that's great, keep that pace going.

Jenny: How long for though?

John: Is Sarah there? Fetch Sarah.

Sam: John, are you alright mate?

John: Fetch Sarah, Sam!

Sam: Alright, alright. Sarah, love! You wanna just come up here a minute, say hello to Granddad? What's this about John?

John: Nothing short of a miracle Sam, nothing short of a miracle. Can you see outside?

Sam: Yeah. We're in the bedroom. It's dark outside. Like middle-of-the-night dark.

John: Good, good. Just watch it though. Keep watching it.

Sarah: Hiya Granddad.

John: Sarah love! Hello my sweetheart, how are you?

Sarah: I'm good thank you. Are you still sad?

Jenny: Sarah...

John: No, no thank you Sarah, but no. I'm as happy as can be! Sarah, listen very carefully – do you have any fruit in the house? Apples or something?

Jenny: We got those bananas didn't we love?

Sarah: Bananas.

John: Perfect! You think you can run and fetch one of those bananas for me?

Sarah: For here? Like, bring it here?

John: Yes, yes! Quick as you can.

Sarah: Ok.

Jenny: Careful on the stairs Sarah, don't run. Why is it dark, Dad?

John: You'll see, you'll see. Oh! My, my, it's working, it's really...oh God!

Jenny: Dad? Dad what is it? What's working?

John: Sorry, pet...it's just...it's really happening...

Jenny: What is? Where are you?

Sam: Come on John, you've got to clue us in here.

John: Ok, sorry. Listen. We've been going at it, a team of us, since one in the morning. Last night. Well, tomorrow, next week, whenever it is!

Jenny: What do you mean Dad? Have you been out all night? Up all night?

Sam: Have you been drinking, John?

John: No, no; clean as a whistle, Sam, don't you worry! I'm fine – I'm more than fine, I'm spectacular. We're all here, the whole group.

Jenny: Who are? What group?

John: Never mind about that, it's a sort of club. A society. It doesn't matter. We've been at this all night, all together – and around the world too. All synchronised.

Sarah: Banana.

John: Sarah! Great, you've got it?

Sarah: Yep. One banana.

John: Ok, put it down on the bed. What colour is it?

Sarah: Yellow.

John: Is all of it yellow?

Sarah: The top bit is a bit green.

Jenny: Sarah, is this from the fruit bowl?

Sarah: Yep.

Jenny: From the ones we bought yesterday in the shop?

Sarah: Yeah, Mummy. What?

Jenny: I bought those bananas cheap. Past their best.

John: Keep watching the banana! Are you still turning Jenny?

Jenny: Yes, I'm turning, I'm turning.

Sam: It's getting light out.

John: Yes, Sam! And it looks like…

Sam: Evening.

John: Bingo! What colour is the banana Sarah?

Sarah: It's going green!

John: Green!

Jenny: Dad what is this? What's going on? I don't like it!

John: Turning back time Jenny, turning back time! We've been at it since one in the morning so we're actually a bit further back than you might think –

Sam: What the hell do you mean John?

John: You can see it! The banana, look. It's back to – maybe four days ago? It'll get faster as you catch up with us.

Jenny: What do you mean catch up, Dad? How far back are you?

John: If the synch has gone right… we'll be coming up to twelve days back now.

Sam: Twelve days?!

Sarah: Are we time-travelling?

John: That's right Sarah! Time-travel, like Doctor Who! Just for a bit though, not forever.

Sam: This is stupid. This is impossible. Jen, put the clock down.

John: Keep turning Jenny.

Jenny: I am Dad. Just tell me when.

Sam: Jen, what the fuck?

Sarah: Daddy!

Sam: Jen, put the bloody clock down.

Sarah: No mummy, keep going!

John: That's right pet, keep going. Keep on…oh God, that's it… keep on turning!

Sam: No. No way. This isn't right.

Jenny: Shut up Sam. Just tell me when Dad.

John: I will pet, I will.

Sam: No fucking way.

Jenny: Stop swearing Sam.

Sarah: Stop swearing Daddy!

Sam: Twelve days? Are you at the cemetery John?

Sarah: The banana is tiny now Granddad. Just a little green stick.

Sam: Answer me John.

John: Yes, Sam, yes. It's working.

Jenny: Is it working, Dad?

John: It's working pet.

Sam: I can't… I can't be a part of this.

John: What's it looking like outside Sam?

Sam: Dark, light. Dark again. Light.

John: You're catching up. It'll slow down soon. Oh my, here we go…

Sarah: Is Granddad at the cemetery Mummy?

Jenny: Yes love. Yes, he is. Dad?

John: …

Sarah: Granddad?

John: …

Jenny: Dad, answer me. Has it worked?

John: …

Jenny: Dad?

John: I'm here, I'm here. Are you ready for this?

Sam: No way in hell, Jen, no way.

Jenny: Shut up, Sam. I'm ready Dad. We're ready.

John: Gladys? Gladys? I've got Jen on the phone. With Sarah. They'd like to say hello.

Four Beaches
Rob Schofield

For six months, Hassan worked as a night porter at the Grand Palace Hotel in Tartus, signing in as the sun set and escaping to his room when it rose the following day. Even in this country, where you could rely upon nothing and nobody – betrayal and bombs, death and suffering aside – you could rely upon the sun to rise.

For six months, Hassan took off his suit every morning and headed to the water. A section of the beach had been partitioned for the foreign tourists – mostly government contractors and journalists – and visiting dignitaries from friendly countries. More often than not, this prime spot was empty. Armed guards from the Ministry of Tourism were always on hand, in shirt sleeves and sunglasses, whispering into walkie-talkies and polishing their automatic rifles. As he swam back and forth in parallel to the beach, beyond the floating boundary, Hassan got to know each one of the guards by their facial tics and moustaches. A couple of them also worked as close protection for some of the visiting Americans. They might have been moonlighting. There was never any nod or word of recognition.

Swimming was a chore. It was boring after ten, twenty minutes. After three hours, it was agonising. After four, it was dangerous. As much as the water itself, Hassan's enemy was cramp and fatigue. But as the proverb says, *patience is the key to relief.* And relief, when it was finally in sight, would be around six kilometres away. Hassan did not know anyone who had ever swum that far. Early one morning, before the guards arrived, he paced out his swim at around two hundred metres. Five lengths, which took him approximately thirty minutes, equalled one kilometre. Six kilometres equalled one hundred and eighty minutes: three hours. After six months he was able to manage four hours in the water, by alternating strokes, occasionally swimming on his back, and sometimes treading water. Four hours would be enough.

After another six months he arrived in Bodrum. He journeyed north, avoiding Aleppo, then onwards to the Oncupinar border crossing, where a returning refugee sold him – at great expense – his Turkish papers. With the help of other Syrians, in particular the brothers who took him in when he fell sick, he walked, hitched and stowed his way to the Turkish Aegean. He had lost too much weight, and he had no money to pay for a boat. He borrowed a few coins to buy a notebook and some pencils, to earn a little money selling sketches and portraits. He built sandcastles and sculptures and offered an upturned baseball cap to the English and German tourists who stopped to admire his work. But there was only ever enough to buy food. There would never be enough for the traffickers.

He left at dawn on his first attempt. He stowed his toiletries, shoes, clothes and notebooks in a plastic bag, wrapped in another plastic bag, inside his backpack. He pulled the pack over his shoulders, clipped the straps around his chest and stomach and walked into the sea. He heard laughter and shouting from the others who were camped along the beach. 'Don't be a fool,' someone said. 'You'll never make it. It can't be done.' A child cried out 'Look Mama, he's wearing his underpants.' But he made good progress. He could see the tip of Kos when he looked up. If those grinning Italians – if they had been English he might have been able to explain – hadn't dragged him out of the water and taken him back to the beach, he could have made it. The next time it was the Coast Guard or the Navy – some kind of uniform – and he would have been in trouble if he hadn't run off when they landed at the harbour, sprinting like a fool along the jetty, a crazy man in pants waking the tourists from their slumber below decks. The third time, he was buzzed by idiots on jet skis. No. Daytime was no good.

It took another three weeks of sketches, portraits and sculptures before he could buy the right head torch and compass. The shopkeeper assured him they were both waterproof. He did not ask if they could withstand the ocean. If and when the light went out, *his strength would be the measure of his desire.* As the day began to fade, he sat down on the beach to eat the few scraps of food he had left. He took off his clothes and packed his bag. Fixing the torch as tight as he could stand, he took a bearing with the compass and tied it around his neck. As he mumbled one final prayer, a voice behind him shouted 'Hey, underpant man!' A woman, with a toddler on her hip, walked towards him. She was pulling a small inflatable dinghy behind her. 'If you must try again, take this.' The dinghy landed at his feet. 'Tie it to your pack. It will help you float.' How could he turn down her gift? So there he was, a skinny man breaststroking towards a bloody horizon, the sun setting below the mountains to one side. The inflatable followed, like a taunt that would not be shaken off.

*

The single bed was pushed against a wall so thin he knew how much his neighbour missed his mother. There was a small wooden table and foldaway chair under the window and a slim wardrobe in one corner behind the door. There was no key for the door. Before he went to sleep he jammed a rubber wedge under the bottom, and moved the table in front of it. His pencils went missing shortly after he moved in, so he carried as much as he could in his backpack whenever he braved the streets. He ferried boxes and crates from stall to stall at a nearby market: fish, meat, vegetables and fruit. The stallholders palmed him coins or filled bags with the produce customers would not buy. He had learned very early on that thirty six pounds and ninety five pence was not enough to live on. He was not allowed to work while he awaited the decision on his claim; and when the middle men laughed at the amounts he tried to send home, he tightened his fists and held his tongue. But there was at least a familiar energy to the market. And the men behind the stalls shouted, laughed and sang all day, teasing old women and chatting up the young ones. What was *Oi! Oi!?* It certainly wasn't covered in the classes at University.

He was planning what to do with the aubergines and courgettes in his carrier bag when he was yanked between two stalls and shoved against a wall. A red haired man with yellow teeth pressed all his weight through his palm against Hassan's chest. A young man with brownish fluff sprouting from his chin stood five paces back, looking at his shoes. This young man would be carrying the boxes from now on. Yet again, Hassan was told to 'Fuck off back to where you came from'. Instead, he took to walking by the river, where one day he leaned over the railings to admire a strip of sand on the otherwise muddy beach that had been unveiled by the ebbing tide.

In Poundland in the Elephant and Castle shopping centre, he bought a child's bucket and spade and some Union Jack bunting. He consulted the tide tables at the local library and arrived at the river late morning. He tied the bucket to the railing and climbed down the ladder to the river beach, where he planted a length of driftwood like a flag on the moon. He fixed one end of the bunting to the railing, looped it around the driftwood and knotted the other end further along. Inside this triangle, he knelt and started to dig. He checked his watch and began to shape the first of two piles of sand. Coins were dropped into the plastic bucket long before he had finished, three hours later. 'Thank you! Thank you,' he shouted over his shoulder, smoothing the sand with a wet hand and allowing himself a smile. He found a stone heavy enough to stop his deflated dinghy afrom blowing away. He walked backwards to the ladder, turned, and climbed up over the railings.

The Chinese tourists looked down, said nothing, and walked away. The Russians, dripping with confidence and money, shouted insults. The Spanish schoolchildren shook his hand, and offered him sweets and cigarettes. As the crumbling parliament building and the city's glass towers faded with the light, the young students urged him down to the beach to take his photograph alongside his sculptures: a man, naked except for his undershorts, clinging to an airless dinghy; and the body of a toddler, face down in the mud, oblivious to the encroaching tide.

On the Evening Train
Fiona Salter

'Your role has been made redundant.' The office reeled back beneath me. I was vaguely aware of muffled sobbing in corners, urgent whispering and, most irritating, the affected concern. What more could you expect from the not-quite friends?

'Will you be ok?' I mumbled something reassuring, but a phrase repeated itself in my stunned brain.

What now?

Change. I abhor it. For twenty years this had been my life – working hard to avoid promotion, neither ambitious nor demanding, just happy to be part of something, which consisted of my special mug, the cakes on Friday, and the wedding, new baby, good luck cards which I signed, but did not receive. My surrogate family, if you were playing the amateur psychology card.

Until now. Ask not for whom the leaving collection tolls.

After the final day, the perfunctory speech – 'like being at your own funeral' whispered a colleague – my manager struggling and failing to find hilarious anecdotes from my 20 years, and so falling back on my 'sterling service'. I accepted the vouchers (M&S, nice and safe) and went home, my bag bulging with files. For what? Filing? I might as well have filed myself while I was at it.

That first week was a drowning. The weather concurred and day turned to dusk.

It was a Victorian rain, cloaking everything, trees, buildings, the throats of commuters – leaving us groping and floundering through familiar streets. Fanciful commentators said it echoed our national malaise, the aftermath of a bruising political storm which had brought in its wake stagnation and blotted out the future.

The Today programme continued to wake me up every morning. I got out of bed, stood at the window and thought: *what now?*

The absence of work gnawed at me like a fox at a carcass. I found myself making a packed lunch for a day that had no need of one. So I looked for comfort in the only place I knew.

The station.

As I neared it I felt a little flutter of familiarity at the bouquet of diesel, sweat, perfume, makeup and newsprint – the smell of the working world. From the footbridge I watched commuters drizzling onto the London-bound platform, standing in little clots at their appointed position. Dead-eyed, unspeaking. Oh, how I longed to join them.

There was a strike in force when I started travelling again. I had nowhere to be, so the strike made no odds. I just slid through the barrier and took my place among them and looked out of sluiced windows.

At my leaving 'do', our IT guy, a bit of a wag, asked about my love life – I noticed my colleagues hold their breath. With a cheerful lack of social awareness, he ignored my glacial stare and insisted 'all I needed' was this app. Sure enough, as the train carried me home I saw it winking at me from my screen. He had installed it on my phone anyway.

I'll give him credit. He knew me well enough to know that I liked the patterns and the beautiful logic of the network. Perfect voyeurism for commuters. The algorithm works out when your paths cross, and presents you with a profile. It felt like stalking. 'Tom is now 1 km away from you', 'now 20 km' as the train carried the smiling Tom back – presumably to his blissfully unaware wife and kids.

'You've crossed paths 11 times' Why not send him a wink, asked the app.

A profile flickered up, and before I swiped, I was arrested by shark eyes. He was balding, with dark wispy tonsure of hair and patchy grey beard. Black frockcoat, rumpled and rolled-up sleeves. No shirt visible under it. What does he think he looks like?

He liked being in the mountains. Not conquering them or abseiling down them like prat, just being in them. I liked that.

The 'I'm looking for' section read simply: 'A fellow traveller'.

I sent him a 'wink' – though in real world I have never winked at anyone or thing, and a question. *Hi, what do you do?*

Let us not dwell on such things, he replied.

Something about his archaic phrasing and his Transylvanian roadie get-up made my flesh creep, a mixture of revulsion and affinity.

That was not altogether a bad thing.

Have you never woken up next to someone and wondered: why? An intersection of pleasure, puzzlement and pain.

One might describe my commuting similarly. I caught the evening train from my non-job and folded myself into Southern Rail's fickle embrace.

Where did I go? Without an income I sought out free sanctuaries, so I haunted galleries, cloisters and parks.

And all the while the sky thickened and clotted, it was like being trapped in Tupperware.

The black rain smelt of soot and vinegar in those dusk days of summer, and seemed to manifest a meteorological PMT, culminating in window-rattling storms that did nothing to release the tension. Even the annoyingly cheerful TV weather woman called it 'apocalyptic'.

On those twilight jobless journeys my laptop sat unopened in front of me, applications waiting to be filled. It all seemed so futile, compared to the intoxicating thrill of swiping profiles.

A woman's face popped up. I could have sworn I had specified I was looking for a man. Yet here was a young black woman with the same direct gaze as the frockcoated man. Oddly, for a dating profile, she held a swaddled baby in her arms, its face turned away from the camera.

She stated: 'Looking for a fellow traveller.'

Hair stood up on my forearms. The same line as the man.

Last week I was checking his profile when I saw its incarnation appear opposite me.

He was reading a book, leather bound. In a carriage of crystal-covered kindles and flickering screens it seemed deliberately affected. The leather had a whiff of formaldehyde. He looked, if not unkempt, then a little moth-eaten, the dust gathered in the folds of the black jacket and on the peak of a cap beside him. His eyes quivered, lips mechanically moved. Then gaze snapped up – startlingly light and intense – and caught me.

'We've met.' I said, 'Well at least online.'

'We have, haven't we?'

That was it, he closed his eyes.

The train juddered to a halt, lightning had struck the line. The other passengers tutted and rolled their eyes, while the rain lashed the windows and the guard prowled the train – a vampire looking for a vein.

My companion flickered his reptile eyes and asked him,

'Whither is this train bound?' The guard swivelled round like a sceptical owl.

'Yer what?'

I felt duty-bound to translate. 'He means where's it going?'

'East Croydon, mate.'

'Have you met anyone nice?' I asked, to fill silence. He didn't smile.

'I've met you, and her,' he indicated the black woman sitting a few seats away, looking directly at us while absently stroking her baby's lifeless back.

I bet she was dreading being stuck here. Nowhere to feed a soon-to-be bawling child on this crowded carriage. But the baby was silent, and I realised with a lurch, unmoving. It was a 're-born' – lifelike with its blue veins and mottled, screwed-up old-man face – distinguishable from the real thing only by its utter and complete silence. I tried not to stare. And couldn't understand why others weren't staring, had no one noticed? Then she slowly turned and met my gaze directly.

Had the trains always been populated with these freaks?

I remembered a quote from Freud: about the uncanny. 'A class of frightening which leads back to what is known of old and long familiar.'

'Though nice,' he said, 'is not a word I care for.'

'I'd better go,' I said.

'Where else do you have to be?'

He patted the seat next to him.

I felt sudden comfort and an odd feeling of 'belonging'. I sat beside him, absorbing his strength, like a plant absorbs light.

My life is divided into BC and AC – before and after commuting. Before I applied for jobs, replied to emails. Today I discover, amazingly, I am shortlisted for interview, they have been trying to call it says. I press delete. I don't have time for an interview, still less a job.

Nor friends – I swipe past texts and missed calls, until they dwindle to radio silence.

My fellow travellers. Exiles from work, society. From life. We travel but never quite arrive.

I sometimes wonder if the guard realises we don't alight at the terminal. If he does he never says anything – but then I wonder about him too.

We have nothing in common with civilians, as we call them, the commuters with a desk waiting for them, with their prattle and purpose.

One cannot bear too much reality. And so we prefer to remain with our own kind.

How many are we, I wonder? I imagine us spreading through the veins of the network, beyond to the Midlands and the North like barium meal on an x-ray. One day I'll travel beyond my commute and discover more of my tribe.

But first, I have a train to catch.

At Sky's Edge
Helen Slavin

In the village there were only a handful of people who knew of Sky's Edge. They were all women. They all hoarded the secret.

In September there had been that trouble with the railmen, come with sleepers and sledgehammers to drive the way through from the City. They had maps and sextants and measuring, but the land had the measure of them.

They stayed at Hind's Hill Farm and the farmer's wife had pocketed their gold gladly. It was the dairy maid, Nora Wheatear who had shaken her head.

'The bog is hungry,' she'd warned and the railmen had been amused. She was pretty with her white skin and her black hair.

The bog drank them in like best bitter.

In October a man had come to the Inn, asking the way to Sky's Edge.

'There's Top Edge and Far Edge?' the landlord suggested, indicating a painted map framed on the wall above the hearth. It was more picturesque than topographical. The man, soaked from the rainstorm raging outside, sank a little at the news he had taken such a wrong turning.

'Pint of your best.' He watched the liquor poured, then downed it fast.

At the hearth, Kitty Bloodstone knitted. Socks or some such. The needles clicked like bones.

On the road once more, the stranger found the rain had waited for him, that the paths he took twisted at his ankles or were impassable and flooded out. He was all ravelled up with cold by the time he found his way to the road that reached the Town.

In November there had been that spooked horse wandering riderless by the mill. It was Martha Dreadnought had found the lost rider all spinny-headed at the crossroads. They'd put him on the waggon to Town. Martha kept the horse safe for the rider, but he did not return.

December turned up bareboned and white with frost. The women of the village who knew, the ones who held the secret in baskets and crocks and candleboxes, waited for the moment. Day struggled with night. The Dusk was coming.

There ought to have been preparations, a gathering of lace or linen, some stitching and embroidery to embellish a gown here, a stocking there. Instead the work they busied themselves with was on account of others. The Ladies who were coming to the Hall demanded beadwork, and baking. The silks that came in through the gates of the Hall were cut and pinned to the forms of others. Boots were fashioned from kidskin, gloves from silk velvet, blankets were woven in the mill for the carriage rides. Silver was polished. Crystal ware and crockery was dusted off.

In the dairy the cheeses were ripening, the butter thickened to yellow gold. Cream cooled in the wide dishes on the sill.

May was his Lordship's newest acquisition. A froufrou delicacy of young womanhood with thousands a year and coal rich estates in Wales, if her father didn't outlive her. There was a chance, after all, his Lordship's first wife, Lady Catherine had died young, the child coming before its time and taking her with it.

'May's strong. A brood mare,' had been her father's recommendation as they shook hands on the nuptial deal. A bargain, for May was light and wild, where Catherine had been serious and sour.

She was not to be tamed, this May, but his Lordship relished the challenge.

'Come.' Her grandmother had taken her to one side, a small

sitting room at her Chelsea home, lined with books. 'You need to learn of women's ways, my dearest.' There were herbs and liquors in a cabinet. A notebook of measures and recipes and May was a keen and clever student. None of her grandmother's recipes called for a kitchen, May understood that with a wry smile.

May and her Lordship had come out of London and driven a long and bumpy road. The towns had given way to smaller towns and then villages and then at last they gave up the ghost and all that was left was the moorland, the slow rising hills. Before the Hall and its village there was one last town, a thin patchwork of streets crowded round a tavern, a butcher's shop, a scuttling little haberdashery and hardware shop.

'How do we manage?' May asked as they trundled through to the far end of Town. 'Do you have livestock at the Hall?' She had a bucolic image of Highland cows in her head although the Hall was not nearly far enough north for that. His Lordship smiled.

'There's the walled garden. And the deer in the park.'

May's eyes glinted a little, setting fires in his Lordship. She leaned across the carriage, resting her hands on his thighs.

'Can we hunt?' she asked, knowing he would grant her anything.

The day of the hunt dawned misty and chill but May was not to be dissuaded. The horses clattered out of the stable yard, the keepers ahead tracking the deer to be certain of a kill.

It did not turn out the way that his Lordship had wanted. The deer were skittish. His friends complained that the weather was too cold.

'You indulge her,' Vickery had smirked as he sipped a toddy at lunch.

'Spare the rod…' Belton began.

'Oh I doubt he spares her that.' The joke filtered through the brandied breath that was clouding the air. His Lordship signalled to the grooms. It was time to return.

May was content. The horse ride alone had been a welcome distraction from the frowsty company. The hunting party made its way over the parkland. Not all the women had ridden out, but those that had were now easily distracted, taken with the sight of the Temple to Apollo, the sculpted stone standing out like a beacon against the ochre and rust of the moorland beyond the walls.

It was May who saw the beast, antlered, racing its way across the shoreline of the ornamental lake. Hooves pounding to a heartstopping leap over the distant gate.

'HO!' she raised her arm, the small black glove reaching to the sky. Some looked with disinterest at the fleeing stag. May turned to her Lordship, her horse jolting and eager beneath her. His Lordship shook his head. May, with that glint in her eye, kicked her heels. As the horse charged off the wind caught at her hat, threw it down in the grass, still she did not halt.

'After her,' his Lordship growled beneath the disapprobation of his friends. The grooms were mounting, gave chase. 'On pain of dismissal,' he shouted at their retreating forms.

He waited many hours before the fire. Supper came and went without him and it was after midnight when the door to his study opened.

The stag's head was to be mounted. The next morning the trophy lay on the mahogany table in the hallway so that all might see it. His wife's kill. He relished their disapproval, their griping jealousy. Their wives: trinkets, bloodless.

'Perhaps we might never go back to London,' May mused, the scent of her hair, blood and earth, intoxicating him.

Solstice. Day meets Night and one is defeated. Dusk comes with her cloak.

At the Hall the ball was glittering and gold. His Lordship watched the way they watched his wife. Her gown, silken and green as a forest to match the emeralds he'd had sent from his bank.

Sweat beaded like diamonds on her lip as they danced. The whirl of light and fiddle and whisky.

Outside, the women who knew, the women who kept the secret, gathered at the edges.

Kitty pulled up her cloak of ivy, carried a basket of freshly spun skeins. Martha rode her horse, bringing a message in the weave of a blanket. Nora brought cream and cheese hidden beneath her coat of bracken.

May took the pins from her hair as she made her way across the garden to meet them, at the farthest edge of the walled garden she tugged on her coat of newly turned earth. She had been shown Sky's Edge in the eye of the deer and knew the way. There was still time.

Kitty, Martha and Nora were only a little ahead of her, slowing their pace so that she might catch up.

Dusk was stepping towards them, her cloak trailing over the moor, blinking out the windows at the Hall, moving to greet them, to take them with her over to Sky's Edge.

May followed, her hand hidden in her pocket, sticky with her offering – the deer's heart.

The Dusk Runner
Cath Bore

She knows full well that winter is gritty and grim for some. Fuel bills are steeper, and everyone goes around swaddled in thick jumpers, long coats biting ankles. Yet she herself enjoys the feel of hard goose bump lumps prickling her arms, the frost pinching her neck. She keeps it quiet but there's nothing quite like the sharp cut of the chill. There's a pleasure in the cold, her mind brightens and clears, thoughts cleaned and polished and sharp. Everything is so precise.

At teatime, nearly time, she settles by the front window, a china cup – plus saucer – on her lap, curtains in the windows open wide, the embroidered white nets veiling her face. The street is a cool grey but with a silvery sheen, save for the soft glow of street lamps clicking on, one by one. Rush hour is over, kids home from school, cars are parked, neat and tidy, and everyone is locked in their homes, done for the day. It is beautiful. There's a comfort in the quiet. It's safe. Nothing is out there, no one.

Apart from him, the one she waits for, all day. Her stomach squirms in delight at the slap-slap-slap of his feet on the pavement. He flashes into view. He runs at dusk, every night. Like an old film on the telly, the hopeful moon makes him Cary Grant, in running shorts and a t-shirt. Cary Grant, for eight seconds. But it's a good eight seconds, of just her, and him. Her neck creases in a barley sugar twist as he goes past, and she savours the sweetness of it. This, here and now, is the best part of the day.

But time moves on and ruins everything. It always does, the New Year comes, the weeks turn into months and March is here, soon enough. Temperatures rise, and everything changes. Every night she takes her seat and watches and hopes, but on 1st April feels the fool. The spring day stretches out, and he does too, running later, longer, and slower. He gains a longer lope, arms bent at the elbow and held low. The sun stays up to warm his pale cheeks pink, he goes from fuzzy charcoal to full colour. The daffodils come, blazes of hysterical yellow. She hates it, all this, the changes, the day the first buds spring, tiny slits of yellow behind folds of green, ready to burst. The air clings and prickles, sweat stretches and flattens her pores. Soon, summer is here. It brings so much bloody noise with it, people milling about in the street, watching him, looking at him. It means she has to share him. And because of the summer, he runs later and later, sunset shifting, pulling him along with it. At the season's peak, the night is so short it's stolen. He squints at her window, lines furrowing his forehead. He holds a cupped hand over his eyes to protect them from the sun then he's off, running away, the daylight snapping at his heels.

Threshold

Katerina Watson

The water stain on the doormat is getting worse. Mottled. She should probably change it.

Should.

Well if we're going doing down should, then there *should* be a key in her hand. That key *should* then go into the lock.

She knows that.

Light streams through the glass panels at the top of her door – their door – *the* door – onto her shoes. She hates them. Maybe she should change them too, maybe she should –

Breathe.

The dusk is creeping in around her outside, on the inside too. Beyond the door he's there, home.

Breathe.

Now don't me wrong. She loves him. Deeply. And he her. It's not about that. No it's about something else.

It's about, it's about what colour the dusk is brewing, right now, in the sitting room. Outside its punch drunk purple shot with streaks of worried grey. Doesn't bode well.

Inside it's...who knows. Yesterday when she arrived at dusk as she always does, tired and bent out of shape herself, she held his head in her hands while he cried. The day before was different of course. The day before he had blotted her out. Not unkindly, not purposefully. But still. As soon as she walked through the door she saw it. He had backed away into that unreachable place, where he hears her voice like she's underwater. One of them's drowning, maybe both.

The day before that? She's tired, who knows. She has vague far off memories of what seemed like an endless summer *but*.

Clear skies can be deceiving. She knows that now too.

Of course, that's not what anyone, everyone, sees.

All day he gets consumed. Online. On TV. Magazines. Once she even saw his face on the side of a bus while an autistic teenager wiped his nose on her sleeve. Her day job. And his.

I just really feel we have a connection!

One of the fans wrote.

Like, we really know each other.

Do you. Really. Because every day she walks in, the dusk is a different colour. Sometimes he's a storm of heavy grey, sometimes the dusk has set in early and has stamped out all the strips of light with darkness. Blank.

But.

Sometimes, just sometimes, she walks through the door and he's *reds* with *pinks* and *oranges* shot through. *Luminous.* Sure there's darkness, there's always darkness, but there are a hundred million stars pinned to his night sky and anything is possible.

Those nights.

Those nights are the best.

So.

She puts her key in the lock. And turns it.

Cape Cornwall
Jackie Taylor

'Meet me at Cape Cornwall – dusk, tomorrow,' he said, and no doubt he had a particular time in mind when he said it, something to do with the angle of the sun on the horizon, something fixed and factual and scientific. But I wasn't sure exactly what time he meant.

There's that time when the sky is streaked red and orange and is all lit from the top, and then you turn around and everything's gone dark behind you without you even noticing, and the old engine houses lean forward out of the twilight. Did he mean that time? When the earth seems to stop breathing, and – briefly – pause?

Or the time when the gulls finally head for the cliffs, and you see the last boat heading for safe harbour round the Cape, and you shiver, however well-dressed you are, knowing that the night is coming? The time when the winter sun gives up its final gasp of warmth and the temperature plummets as straight and true as a mine shaft, and the wind whips up as cold as lead off the sea. Is that when he meant?

Or did he mean the time when you can't see the cliff-edge any more, or the sheer drop to the sea? When you can't see where the path has crumbled away, or where an old shaft has opened up after the rain?

'Meet me at Cape Cornwall – dusk, tomorrow.' But I didn't know what time he meant, not exactly.

Maybe he meant that time when the light starts to fail, and talk turns to scaling down the search. When cups of tea and blankets are brought out for the search teams, and everyone knows there's no hope, but no-one wants to be the first to say it out loud.

Or perhaps he meant that particular time when the search is finally, reluctantly, called off, and the lifeboat is recalled, and you watch it heading for safe harbour around the Cape as darkness falls around you.

POEMS

Gloaming
Mandy Macdonald

the air darkening, after rain
no, don't move, not yet
the moment held fast
so as not to undertake
anything fatal

End of Ramadan
Michelle Penn

Mombasa, Kenya

I could tile rooms with stasis.
A wail could replace my voice
denoting the divisions
        between the bold and the veiled –

        The winding streets of the Arab quarter at dusk:
mosquitoes fight to claim my flesh, I sidestep
buzzing pools, tug the scarf
        closer to my eyes.

My skin calls out, *I am not like you.* It is not faith
        but the hand at my back that nudges me through,
        belonging with it or perhaps to it
a woman, too visible, invisible –

Safety is the pattern built by tiles.
His insistence – just one sting and the body goes weak.

I inch the veil aside
not to court impropriety but to invite
        a sea breeze, catch a solitary chant
        whisper my own prayer
            for this fast to continue – just a bit longer –

The Shortest Day
Sue Johnson

wait at the daylight gate
the gap between the worlds
is thin as a lace curtain

do not be afraid – none will harm you
look for signs of magic
near oak ash and thorn

be aware of crows and ravens
they are the otherworld gatekeepers
sent with messages from loved ones

leave an offering of silver
be thankful for all you have
look for the coming of the light

Factory
Joy Howard

Like sleeping elephants
abandoning the day's march
machines gasp small breaths
into the cooling dark

now for the night-stoop of owls
for the pale-eyed moon
for teeth bared
at the infancy
of human endeavour

After the Sun, Before the Stars
Jane Aldous

I'd promised to be there, before the half-light dimmed,
before the half-dark was summoned or smoke-grey
changed to implacable blue. Already I could distinguish
no colours but white in the Cornus berries, snowy hens,
Cosmos, washing on the line.

But I was late, it was after the sun and before the stars
were revealed and my eyes were taking time to focus.
People were queuing for buses to take them home,
blackbirds were scurrying back to the roost, streetlights
stuttering into life, the temperature was falling.

All the shapes and shadows had merged by the time
I arrived at the gate. But then I saw the glow of torches
being lit and I joined a raggle of illuminated faces.
Someone handed me a book and before the Moon came up
many odes and ballads were read in the lee of Castle Rock.

Lines from *Thomas the Rhymer*, *The Faerie Queen*, Burns,
Scott and *Y Goddodin* were all invoked. We crossed through
the grey, the haar, the half-closed eyes, the curtain coming
down
into the opaque, black ink, the certainty of night.

Decoration of a Fermented Season
Alice Tarbuck

What I am trying to say is that somewhere,
where there is an orchard, a child plunges
her thumb down through rotten flesh to find
the centre of a plum. It is the same core,
hard and ridged, that winter is made of.
Under the leaves, sticky with dark fruit
she knows.
The edges catch as the low sun sinks,
her thumb bleeds
redder than plum-skin, more iron
than tart sugar.
So the winter, because
the orchard is synchronous,
produces sharp channels of frost
along the grass, ices the last of the wasps,
transforms the plums into detritus,
sends her home
in the last light,
with the dark stone
rattling in her shoe.

Tempus Erat

Kate Wise

It was that time of night
when leaf turns bat
and skitters mothing
through bruised air
And Perseus
(who would have me call him Perseus)
skips
stabbing gorgon birch with bamboo spear
But I his mother
dear him Achilles
a pearl that blazed so bright
it would burn itself out
blond; blond and blazing
and worry –
where? Where did I keep hold too tight
when I dipped him in the flow?

Crow Haibun
Alison Lock

Crow lands on a rowan tree in a shiver of feathers. The thrall days of chill are here. Crow feeds on the berries ripened in the sun of a mellow season. Woodsmoke drifts from a stack with barely a tint on a peaty sky. Black on muted – Crow's silhouette is sharp – craw, hood, beak.

> dark-veins fall
> from a copper beech

After the frost the bracken has bleached in the sun, catching the light. Brittle tendrils bristle in the breeze, a rustle to the ear. Crow looks down from the scree and the sky. A single tree stands alone – a skeleton, its thin branches spread.

> through the mist
> a ghost rises.

The texture of bark is a story – times of growth, of dearth, of abundance – with each crease and every fold. From the silver birch an imprint is shed, casting memory to the ground.

> hanging skin,
> papyrus

Leaves quiver like stiff wings caught in the trees. A glimpse of past seasons span the gap. It is dusk in the woods. Only the stalks, twigs, the brown husks filter the dying light.

> a split trunk
> rings meet

Crow takes off, blatting the leaves, cawing as he rises, dropping a stone, a seed to the ground before the lowering sun.

> at the day's end
> deadwood blooms

all this
John Richardson

Can't shake this late love of summer's twilight
that dresses sounds of children, back gardens away
a whisk of midges lifts off the pond into a scythe
of swifts; the swallows all agape, upwing.

The passing light silvers our trees,
and grass already flattered, sighs
over late watering rites, sprinklers
do Mexican waves, and waves

of faint laughter 'luminate the fields,
Summer Nights is being karaokeed out of tune
but we keep the windows open,
welcome what air there is inside

to stir a breath of worry about all this.
Yet – what happens – happens. And
night's sweats throws sheets, curtains,
aside to reveal a cool entertainment:

stars turning on,
and off, just for us.
Then it dawns
that someone,

somewhere,
the latest footfall
on the other side,
has missed

all this.

Starling Time
Laila Sumpton

It's a day for melting earrings
the lull before – to re-heel boots,
bury diaries, cross out your name
from trees.

A day to relish the gleams you gather
as you heft basket and saunter
as if you carry spirals of eel –
which your mother always said
were the hairs or drowned sailors
swimming out of brine to land
as she'd jar their jelly and hum.

Your wicker traps are left open
woven, door-less, sunken homes
harbouring the pretence
that you'll be here tomorrow.
You wring the river from you
and follow her to sea.

A murder and murmur heckle sky,
you watch winged shoals dividing,
unable to roost–
and you know which one you will follow
as summer yearns,
as towers beg you to kneel,
as net stitcher gleams shrivel to glints
you walk on under the evening star,
dropping your key in the sand.

Match Girl
Lisa Kelly

*Most terribly cold it was; it snowed, and was nearly quite dark, and evening –
the last evening of the year.*

Hans Christian Andersen

I.

In this story, you're on the inside
while outside, dusk begins to nibble,
then opens its black mouth and swallows
light in one greedy gulp. Never mind.
You can gorge on goose. That time of year
when food is hearty and the hearth roars,
family forgiven, foes ignored.
You sink tired feet in fluffy slippers
with reindeer faces, and crack walnuts
for the divertissement of plying
a silver tool instead of smoking,
chew on the nuts which cause canker sores.
The Christmas tree shines with candlelight.
Outside, something sparks, flares in the night.

II.

In this story, you're on the outside,
shaking, looking in through misted glass
at a knife and fork stuck in roast goose
which waddles towards you. Never mind.
It is stuffed with apples and dried plums.
You could be a grandma in heaven.
You could be a girl on heroin.
How many matches left? Do the sums.
Make ends meet as phosphorous strikes brick:
a psychedelic trip of colour.
Burning upon green branches, tapers
which fade to nothing, leaving the dark.
Sometimes, you feel up against a wall.
Sometimes, dusk lets you see a star fall.

Summers Ended in Sweetness
Martyn Crucefix

Under the boughs of the oak named Eve
lies a shape
settling its wheels into the turf
as if to say sooner or later all these things

will sink like this wish-bone
of an old farmyard cart
this four-wheeled broken-backed wreck
with its load of inadvertent scraps

in a metal hopper long since blotched
and scorched with rust
now peppered with acorns and twigs
the seasons' debris from the spreading trees

and over the bent rear axle
a barrel-shaped composite of metal hoops
around wooden staves
once clamped to each other to be water-tight

the wood originally young and full
now shrunken–the staves lost wholesale–
and it was here baskets of fruit
were brought to be pressed by the screw

winding down to the metal base
until grape juice spilled from the spout
protruding like an obscene tongue
on which decades of summers ended in sweetness

towards which gangs of children
stretched their hands only to be told to scat
to back off by fathers
who heaved at the wooden cross-struts

like a capstan they looked to squeeze more
and still more oozing sweetness
to drink or decant or spill across the ground–
but now it stands and rots

and bolts lie where they drop
and others wriggle loose to fall perhaps
this winter or next
each heavy square-headed iron bolt

a child might gaze at and think it would last
forever instead only long enough
to be outmoded till this four-wheeled cart
came to a stop one September dusk

was left to stand beneath the boughs
of Adam and Eve when somebody thought
it might prove useful one more year
but they never came back

not the baskets not the hands nor the horses
no tractor returned
and no more the children who sometimes stir
out of their sour old age

to stare down into hands stiff and more used
to a walking frame only to find
palms unwrinkled and a little sticky still
with the taste of six or seven summers

Roost
Sue Birchenough

barely there settles the bus stop, with fingerprints of kids,
just getting bathed

barely hills

the houses are heavy on the day

they land like flying boats
crash and skid the slates like chalk chittering and
squawking –
over pickings, personal space, and the niceties of rank –
when there's half an inch of beak to do the talking

Red Coat, Wolf, etc.
Katy Lee

The soft hush
of air thinning.
A clarity.
Sound has more cadence.
Colour dims.

Depth of field gone,
all is here and now.
Fact and fiction merge.

The wolves' yellow eyes shine out
from the car park,
and my wings itch under my coat.
The red had faded to an off-grey
and I sharpen my teeth on my credit card
picking a tuft of fur from between my molars.

My hard focus has become soft.
My peripheral vision has replaced straight ahead.
My linear has become circular.
I sit and wait for the Woodcutter to arrive.

Roosting birds trade places
jostling for a space to tuck their heads.
The owls and stoats have yet to waken.

A pause.
A rift in time.
A chink,
where disorder and chaos
come tumbling in.
Forbidden thoughts are now permissible
I admit to ones I didn't even know I had,
and you nod in agreement.

And all the while
Grandmother gathers up her bones
places them in a hessian bag
slings it over her back

And walks towards me.

16:30
Katie Evans

At sunset, they cry
in front of the
Gala Bingo's window
at their own discoloured
faces; without the magic
at their fingertips
the break
breaks their spells.
Women smoking together.
Chipping away
at their nails to dig into the
dirt beneath.

Calligraphy of Starlings
Aziz Dixon

Words take wing, lapwing
flocks flocking, word-mocking
geese in skeins fly straight
into the sunset with winter-haunting
cries. Words hover,
drop a few feet with feather-light control,
hover again, kestrel
seeking evening meal, no poem
to eat; but, frog-like, my words
slip away into sedge-safety at dusk,
while a calligraphy of starlings
murmurates, restlessly sweeping the sky
with your name, high
over Limey Water.

Calling Them In

Kelly Davis

'Come home for your tea!'
we called them in, as day fled
and night ate our words.

The sun had already set.
'Come home for your tea!'
Anxiety edged our voices
and night ate our words.

It was much too late.
The sun had already set.
'Come home for your tea!'
Anxiety edged our voices,
imagined fears grew larger
and night ate our words.

They grew up so suddenly.
Dusk took us by surprise.
It was much too late.
'Come home for your tea!'
They could no longer hear us.
The sun had already set,
with darkness at its heels,
and night ate our words.

We were wasting our breath.
It seems a moment ago
but it's twenty years or more.
Somehow they gave us the slip.
Time wouldn't wait.
Did we suspect, even then?
Anxiety edged our voices.
Perhaps we had a premonition –
imagined fears grew larger.
We tried to call them home
and night ate our words.

Summer Evening
Lindsay Reid

A faint pink line of clouds
Settles on the church tower.

In the fragrant summer evening
The thrush is calling.

Darting swallows are silhouetted
Against the sky.

The lights in the library are on –
You are working late.

Step outside into the cool air
And remember who you are.

Afterglow
John Bevan

After light, comes the dark
when flowers fade, foxes bark
children cry, mothers scold.
Am I alone in growing old?

After dark, comes the light
a faded kind, yet so bright;
one that shows me where to go
though where that is, I cannot know.

Some Times a Black Cloud
Nigel Hutchinson

some times a black cloud
some times only ghost of dancers

brushstrokes across a sky, inky scribble
sometimes a black cloud

sometimes only ghost of dancers
brushstrokes across a sky, inky scribble

peppered graffiti in lowering light
hundreds, thousands, tens of thousands

wheeling switchback riders
peppered graffiti in lowering light

hundreds, thousands, tens of thousands
wheeling switchback riders

always one the last to roost
imagine the panic in its heart

Dhusarah
Elizabeth Parker

I
Dusk

is a word
complex as crystal. Tilt it,
find its myriads;
a word
re-worked, re-moulded
but always cool, always smooth;
a word that reached us
through dim passages;
a word
seeded in the mouths of Saxons;
a word
we study under our lamps, our hot bulbs
but only a half-light
reaches fuscus, dox, doxian[1];
a word
grown far from its seeds:
duske, duska[2];
a word bereaved;
a word we have stilled,
forgetting its verbs:
dosk[3], dusken, dusked, dusking.

1 Fuscus: Latin: dark. Dox: Old English: dark-haired/dark/swarthy.
Doxian: Old English: to darken in colour.
2 Duska: Swedish: be misty.
3 Dosk: Middle English: obscure/ to become dark.

Dusk
is a Saxon fort
cupping dark air.

Dusk
is a sound, an echo.
Husk. Musk. Dhusarah[4]. Dust.
Motes, shoals –
see it fall, see it settle –
everything dim
under soft pelts.

Dusk
is stories
read by antique light –
the amber and honey
of whale oil lamps, candles –
stories told as the world gutters,
leaping into the mind,
snuffed.

Dusk
wasn't always blue.

Dusk
was dosan, tusin[5].

---

4 Dhusarah: Sanskrit: dust-coloured.
5 Dosan: Old Saxon: chestnut-brown. Tusin: Old High German: pale yellow.

II
Dusk

is not to be confused
with twilight.

Dusk is scientific,
categorised:
civil, nautical, astronomical.

Dusk
changes its name
as the sun moves below the horizon.

6°
Civil dusk

Enough light to read by,
the day's page still reaching the eye.

A borderline for measuring crime:
years more prison time
if the line is crossed
into burglary by night.

12°
Nautical dusk

Pages are snuffed,
words join the dark,
ink subsumed into ink;

the quiet creak
as we close the day.

Sailors lose the horizon,
down their sextants.

Military initialism: EENT[6]:
End Evening Nautical Twilight.

Even here, in a word
that is barely more than a breath,
there is war – soldiers standing-to
since India and France learnt to hide
whole armies in the half-light.

---

6 EENT is treated with heightened security and this is partly due to the
French and Indian war, part of the Seven Years War, when France and India
would launch attacks at nautical dusk or dawn.

18°
Astronomical dusk

Astrologers' eyes
join up the stars,
draw human shapes on the night.

Our metaphors close the distance:
scattered salt,
the sky mined for diamonds

galaxies, nebulae,
the faintest stars;
the diffuse allowed to shine.

A Female Blackbird Sings

Ness Owen

Ym Mrig y Nos[7]

Your song isn't
as loud as his
born knowing you'll
have to try harder
still you sing not
just with throat but
wings and tail forcing
out your voice like
you're drowning in
the chorus till you
find the one note
to stop them still.
At dusk the order
of chorus reverses
last becomes first
power lies in the
un-expected
they don't recognise
you but at last you
have their ear.

7 Welsh: At Dusk (literally *the edge of the night*)

Driving to Blackpool to Visit my Sister

Jeremy Dixon

I'm thinking of overtaking a hearse
on the A49, five miles outside

Church Stretton, one Thursday
mid-December. A twist of us

at dusk, all cornering far too
fast, impatient for a straightness.

I resolve not to swear again.
Tall headlights rise from a dip

in the carriageway opposite.
I'm guessing it's a tractor, towing

something big, going slow. God.
How long do I have to accelerate?

Magic Hour
Nicholas McGaughey

Blacks crowd the wings,
Blow smoke screens for a magic hour.
Dawn reversed, majesties the
Commonplace:
Sheds, clothes-lines
The monolithic BBQ,
The plastic chairs and tables
Of a workingman's kingdom,
Transformed to a set in the silver-light:
Die Fledermaus? or an opera king
In his court of stars in the orchestra of
Hills with the moon as jester.

Dusk takes its curtain call
With all the golden chorus bowed and left.
House lights blind us back
From the music of the spheres,
From that momentary dream of twilight,
To night-thoughts, and another king
Next-door, singing
On his china throne.
You Were Always on my Mind.
Bass and baritone.

The Sea's Wedding
Carl Griffin

A wedding, or other forms of happiness,
is what happens when you stop obsess-
ing with the life's gems you're not meant
to lust for. Not there to catch a moment,
photographers are brought in to remind you
forever of your decision, resolve. Of you.
I've never married. Never been decisive.
This photographer, big, bald, obtrusive,
is overweight and overbearing. Larger than
the wedding. He doesn't snap a man
or woman or Oxwich bay. He photographs suspects.
It's strange to dress smartly, without specks
of blood-like sauce. Stranger still to toast
your sister. When tonight, Storm Aileen is forecast.

It's sunny enough, though, for photos
as we gather by the fountain and the surly
photographer leans out of the hotel window
telling us where to stand. The shot will be
of fifty people looking up at the sun
with their hand over their eyes, wishing
the photographer would be swung
out of the window. I don't mind admitting
I spend half the wedding avoiding my dad
but a wedding without our heavenly father
seems ironic. I miss being driven mad
by too many hymns, a sermon, an amateur
organist. The couple should brace themselves
for what tonight's storm shakes off the shelves.

I scan the wedding party for possibles.
A bearded teenager in a pink suit
has dressed to stand out in the storm.
Men in pink put me off. The rascal
of my dreams could grind or worm
in this pink get-up and give a cute
come-on and I'd only see contrivance.
But no wedding bells sound or confetti
fall where I tend to walk. A dalliance
should not last as long as the melting
of an ice cube just out of the freezer.
Commitment's an endeavour I've dealt in
only in daydreams. This pink soliloquy,
I'd have his gall in place of my failures.

If you can see a storm then that's all
you can see, pausing the drink to stare
through a marquee window. Out there,
somewhere, is a sea. In the dancehall
I sink into a void like the one staring back.
Where there's only dancing. Flying debris.
Where nothing lands. Later, just us three
singletons are dancing, if you can call it that,
as if the others have sensed for a minute
that in the raging storm something tangible
occurs nearby, a scene which would be visible
on clear nights. But contemplation has its limit
and by the next song everyone's back up
on their feet. Commitment might be enough.

At closing, a few of us dare to walk
onto the beach, stumbling in the wind
which sometimes whips up the sand
but is mostly easing up. A tree has fallen
near the Nature Reserve and is blocking
the road. The roads around here don't fork
for miles. We find a trunk on the beach,
a human one, whaled up it looks like,
unmoving, bearing a hangover he won't wake
up to. It's the photographer, soaking
in the tide not long out, his belly poking
above the fading waves. To reach
a dead man takes longer than you'd think.
Marriages walk on water. Or marriages sink.

Sundown Breath
Gabrielle Choo

The earth casts her nets wide
H O L D T I G H T
She grips each edge of atmosphere
And surely she begins to breathe in
Sucking back the thin skin of sun
That skims across the cities horizon
She unravels each element of the day
Dissolving chatter down swelling windpipes
Melting Monday moments into stories of since
Laying doings and dones to rest in pockets of lungs

She lets go
Sighs out slow
Golden lined pigeons
Pink skies of promise
Lullabies of dinner times
A glimpse of coming home

Arrival
Bridie Toft

An air of quiet in the calm and layered grey,
dogs are straining for the beach.
From the marsh, St. Michael's floats on high tide,
no lights twinkle and the castle waits
modestly.
The marsh is an empty stage of fading sky.
Here they come –
the first small dots above the reeds.

And they come. And they come. And they come.

Squadrons cluster the telegraph lines until
full, they spill back into the sky.
A feathered blizzard morphs,
funnels and arcs in avian ectoplasm,
dips deep into the marsh, absorbed
by browns and shadows.
The bait ball spooks and opens,
a sky-wide wall of birds,
a silvered display in
and out of black.
The wall coils,
a vast centrifuge of beak and wing,
the base peels away, drops down
and the centrifuge unravels.
A circus of sky dives into a sea of reeds.

And it's over.

I am Dusk

Alannah Egan

Temporary incompletion,
I find myself caught.
I am the in-between, suspended in time.
Neither here, nor there; I just am.

A blending of colours,
I attempt to merge.
I am lost in transition,
striving
to become a whole, a definite.

I clasp tightly to the hands of day.
The light peels itself away from me, finger by finger.
I lose all grasp.
Sinking,
Falling,
Tenderly caught by night.

ABOUT THE AUTHORS

With so many authors involved, including biographical notes here would tip the book into another section of sixteen pages. You can find details of *all* our authors and poets on our website: www.arachnepress.com.

ABOUT ARACHNE PRESS

Arachne Press is a micro publisher of (award-winning!) short story and poetry anthologies and collections, novels including a Carnegie Medal nominated young adult novel, and a photographic portrait collection. We are very grateful to Arts Council England for financial support for this book, and to Feast, Cornwall Council, Nottingham City Council, Greenwich Council and all the venues and organisers who supported us with financial and in kind assistance with this year's Solstice Shorts Festival Dusk events.

We are expanding our range all the time, but the short form is our first love. We keep fiction and poetry live, through readings, festivals, our regular event *The Story Sessions*, workshops, exhibitions and all things to do with writing.

Follow us on Twitter:
@ArachnePress
@SolShorts

Like us on Facebook:
ArachnePress
SolsticeShorts2014
TheStorySessions

More from Arachne Press

www.arachnepress.com

BOOKS

All our books (except Poetry) are also available as e-books.

Short Stories

London Lies

ISBN: 978-1-909208-00-1

Our first Liars' League showcase, featuring unlikely tales set in London.

Stations: Short Stories Inspired by the Overground line

ISBN: 978-1-909208-01-8

A story for every station from New Cross, Crystal Palace, and West Croydon at the Southern extremes of the East London branch of the Overground line, all the way to Highbury & Islington.

Lovers' Lies

ISBN: 978-1-909208-02-5

Our second collaboration with Liars' League, bringing the freshness, wit, imagination and passion of their authors to stories of love.

Weird Lies

ISBN: 978-1-909208-10-0

WINNER of the Saboteur2014 Best Anthology Award: our third Liars' League collaboration – more than twenty stories varying in style from tales not out of place in *One Thousand and One Nights* to the completely bemusing.

Solstice Shorts: Sixteen Stories about Time

ISBN: 978-1-909208-23-0

Winning stories from the first *Solstice Shorts Festival* competition together with a story from each of the competition judges.

Mosaic of Air by Cherry Potts

ISBN: 978-1-909208-03-2

Sixteen short stories from a lesbian perspective.

Liberty Tales, Stories & Poems inspired by Magna Carta

ISBN: 978-1-909208-31-5

Because freedom is never out of fashion.

Happy Ending NOT Guaranteed by Liam Hogan
ISBN: 978-1-909208-36-0
Deliciously twisted fantasy stories.
Shortest Day, Longest Night
ISBN: 978-1-909208-28-5
Stories and poems from the *Solstice Shorts Festival* 2015 and 2016.

Poetry

The Other Side of Sleep: Narrative Poems
ISBN: 978-1-909208-18-6
Long, narrative poems by contemporary voices, including Inua Elams, Brian Johnstone, and Kate Foley, whose title poem for the anthology was the winner of the 2014 *Second Light* Long Poem competition.
The Don't Touch Garden by Kate Foley
ISBN: 978-1-909208-19-3
A complex autobiographical collection of poems of adoption and identity, from award-winning poet Kate Foley.
With Paper for Feet by Jennifer A. McGowan
ISBN: 978-1-909208-35-3
Narrative poems based in myth and folk stories from around the world.
Foraging by Joy Howard
ISBN: 978-1-909208-39-1

Poems of nature, human nature and loss.

Novels

Devilskein & Dearlove by Alex Smith
ISBN: 978-1-909208-15-5
NOMINATED FOR THE 2015 CILIP CARNEGIE MEDAL.
A young adult novel set in South Africa. Young Erin Dearlove has lost everything, and is living in a run-down apartment block in Cape Town. Then she has tea with Mr Devilskein, the demon who lives on the top floor, and opens a door into another world.

The Dowry Blade by Cherry Potts

ISBN: 979-1-909208-20-9

When nomad Brede finds a wounded mercenary and the Dowry Blade, she is set on a journey of revenge, love, and loss.

Brat: Book One of *The Naming of Brook Storyteller*

by Ghillian Potts

ISBN: 978-1-909208-41-4

On her twelfth birthday Brat's father disappears. Reduced to begging and determined to find out what has happened to him, she is helped by Gray and Baylock, whom she quickly discovers are outlaws. There is far more to them than a disagreement with the law, and Brat finds that nothing is simple, and nowhere is safe.

Spellbinder: Book Two of *The Naming of Brook Storyteller*

by Ghillian Potts

ISBN: 978-1-909208-46-9

Brook, Brat, Spellbinder… storyteller, remembrancer, witness… with as many names as she has titles, Spellbinder is abducted by Westron Lord Arrow, who holds storytellers as hostages to force her to raise the Elder Dragons, but once they are called, Brook cannot control them.

Forthcoming from Ghillian Potts

Wolftalker, Book Three of *The Naming of Brook Storyteller*

ISBN: 978-1-909208-49-0

Someone is felling gilden trees, the life of the Overlord is threatened, and Storyteller Brook Wolftalker Dragonfriend (known as Brat to her friends) and her new apprentice Cricket, try to unravel who is behind the plot, and more importantly *why*.

Photography

Outcome: LGBT Portraits by Tom Dingley

ISBN: 978-1-909208-26-1

80 full colour photographic portraits of LGBT people with the attributes of their daily life – and a photograph of themselves as a child. @OutcomeLGBT

Events

Arachne Press is enthusiastic about live literature and we make an effort to present our books through readings.

The Solstice Shorts Festival

(http://arachnepress.com/solstice-shorts)

Now in its fourth year, Solstice Shorts is all about time: held on the shortest day of the year on the Prime meridian, stories, poetry and song celebrate the turning of the moon, the changing of the seasons, the motions of the spheres, and clockwork!

We showcase our work and that of others at our own occasional live literature event, in south London: *The Story Sessions,* which we run like a folk club, with headliners and opportunities for the audience to join in (http://arachnepress.com/the-story-sessions) We are always on the lookout for other places to show off, so if you run a bookshop, a literature festival or any other kind of literature venue, get in touch; we'd love to talk to you.

Workshops

We offer writing workshops suitable for writers' groups, literature festivals and evening classes, which are sometimes supported by live music – if you are interested, please get in touch.

Stay in touch:
Twitter @arachnepress
        @solshorts
Facebook www.facebook.com/ArachnePress/
        www.facebook.com/SolsticeShorts2014/
        www.facebook.com/TheStorySessions/